Dreaming
Revolution

Dreaming
Revolution

Transgression in the
Development of American Romance

SCOTT BRADFIELD

University of Iowa Press 🌵 *Iowa City*

University of Iowa Press, Iowa City 52242

Copyright © 1993 by the University of Iowa Press

All rights reserved

Printed in the United States of America

Printed on acid-free paper

Library of Congress Cataloging-in-Publication Data
Bradfield, Scott.

    Dreaming revolution: transgression in the development of American romance / Scott Bradfield.

       p.   cm.

    Includes bibliographical references and index.

    ISBN 0-87745-395-0 (alk. paper)

    1. American fiction—19th century—History and criticism.

2. Politics and literature—United States—History—19th century.

3. Literature and society—United States—History—19th century.

4. Cooper, James Fenimore, 1789–1851—Political and social views.

5. Revolutionary literature, American—History and criticism.

6. Poe, Edgar Allan, 1809–1849—Political and social views.

7. Brown, Charles Brockden, 1771–1810. Edgar Huntly. 8. Godwin, William, 1756–1836. Things as they are. 9. American fiction—European influences. 10. Social conflict in literature.

11. Romanticism—United States. 12. Imperialism in literature.

I. Title.

PS374.P6B7   1993

813'.309358—dc20

                                          92-46717

                                              CIP

97 96 95 94 93 C 5 4 3 2 1

To the memory of my mother,
who made it possible

Contents

Acknowledgments

This book, began as a series of graduate student essays at the University of California, Irvine in 1983, was later developed into a dissertation and then into this book. I owe thanks to the many people who put up with me academically during the last ten years: my dissertation chairman, John Carlos Rowe, along with Bob Maniquis, Christiane Von Buelow, Homer Brown, and Linda Georgiana. To my friends and fellow graduate students I owe a lot of beer and sympathy: Joanne Gass, Lollie Groth, Michael Chabon, Mike and Marla Guista, and Kris Shelton. This book also benefited from readings and comments by Nevil Parker and Alison Hild. And finally, thanks go to the University of Connecticut English Department and the University of Connecticut Research Foundation for their generous support during the past two years of final revisions.

Introduction

Transgression, Michel Foucault argues, "contains nothing negative, but affirms limited being—affirms the limitlessness into
which it leaps as it opens this zone to existence for the first
time."[1] For Foucault, as for Nietzsche, the exemplary philosopher
affirms the "limitlessness" of either humanity or knowledge by
perpetually transgressing boundaries of the known—known laws,
cultures, moralities, governments. Such a philosopher does not
return readers to places they have been but teaches them to overleap those places, misremember and surpass them. Transgression
"is not related to the limit as black to white, the prohibited to
the lawful, the outside to the inside, or as the open area of a
building to its enclosed spaces. Rather, their relationship takes
the form of a spiral which no simple infraction can exhaust"
(35). Transgression is not a finite act so much as an infinite capacity; the limit is not a place so much as a transcendental imperative. By transgressing limits, people discover further limits to
be transgressed. They break laws in order to establish new laws
worth breaking; they progress to a point from which they can
progress again.[2]

In the late eighteenth and early nineteenth centuries, revolutionary Western bourgeois culture instituted the idea that acts of
transgression generate social order, both in terms of political reform and imperial expansion; in other words, transgression began to be conceived of as a disciplinary activity. By transgressing
the authority of aristocratic institutions, revolutionaries could
presumably establish truer, more comprehensive laws and governments; by transgressing foreign territories, they could secure
greater resources for their governments back home. Revolution
disciplined politics, institutions, and people, just as colonial incursions disciplined wildernesses, native cultures, and raw materials. Like revolutionaries, colonists considered themselves part

of that "spiral which no simple infraction can exhaust," a cycle of movement that was always returning home again—with more food, slaves, information, territories, and profits.

The appropriation of foreign lands, like the subversion of aristocratic estates and privileges, reincorporated the perilous "other" within a purportedly vaster and more legitimate scheme of civil society. By crossing foreign borders or invading aristocratic spaces, bourgeois culture dreamed it was democratizing both humanity and the world. Aristocrats were subverted in order to make them democratically virtuous and happy, responsible to a rigorous scheme of social relations they never realized they needed before. Likewise American Indians—envisioned as spiritually isolated and self-sufficient, atomic, random, irrational, guerrilla— were robbed of land in order to be brought into a community of international commerce that would make both them and their land more valuable and productive. By transgressing American space, Europeans never simply reshaped the places they were going but reimagined the places they had been.

Traditionally, Euro-American literature has been depicted as a sort of cultural renegade, one which breaks from Europe to institute a "free space" where "New Adams" regain their innocence, releasing American culture from any political obligations to either Europe or the past.[3] This vision of a renegade America has informed American literary criticism well into the twentieth century. From Richard Chase through Michael Davitt Bell, the American "romance" has always been considered a transgressive generic act. For Chase, it describes an imaginative journey away from the mundane realities of class, history, and politics; it breaks from the realistic "tradition" of the European novel by opening itself to the wider imaginative territories of "mythic, allegorical and symbolistic forms."[4] American romance journeys beyond the merely known into the infinitely possible, teaching readers to appreciate a "circuit of life" that extends their knowledge "through the real and the ideal, through the directly known and the mysterious or the indirectly known, through doing and feeling" (27). More recently, Michael Davitt Bell identifies the romance by its "moral irresponsibility," its refusal to present useful facts or moral lessons. Instead of telling readers about real events or exemplary lives, the romance, Bell argues, provides "the spurious and possibly dangerous as opposed to the genuine."[5]

From Chase to Bell, or Fiedler to Lewis, American romance is
traditionally held up as a model of cultural and geographical independence, a place people journey toward in order to become
more free. By venturing beyond the mundane realism of European novels, American romance colonizes the unknown and describes the inexpressible.[6]

In the following chapters, however, I will argue that Europeans never found a "free space" in the New World because they
took too many Old World stories along with them to light the
way. By presuming to "transgress" European laws and traditions,
Americans acted out a story originally generated by class conflict
in Europe. European stories were not abandoned, they were recoded. American novelists did not create new stories so much as
recontextualize old ones. I will argue that this transatlantic recoding altered the conceptual meaning of transgression in three
significant ways:

1. A story describing how humble, self-educated, underprivi-
leged bourgeois men subvert aristocratic injustice becomes translated into a story about transgressing not only British hegemony
but foreign lands and people. As a result, the conflict between
Democratic Individual and Privileged Aristocrat becomes refig-
ured as a conflict between the European and the Native American, or between Colonial Adventurer and Western Wilderness.

2. This refiguring of the political into the imperial marks the
translation of political tropes into psychological ones. The domain of class interests and political landscapes becomes interior-
ized as a battle between the uncivilized Indian and the civilized
European. A division of races becomes remetaphorized as a division of self.

3. Even while certain structural oppositions are recoded and
redeployed, they never entirely repress the class conflict that first
struck them into existence. No matter how far into the wilderness
American narrative ventures, the figure of the aristocrat continues to haunt its imaginative life.

As Henry Nash Smith argues in *Virgin Land*, America went
west in order to establish a permanent revolutionary victory over
Britain, driving its pioneers toward the Pacific to usurp British
naval and mercantile superiority; by defining new trade routes,
they could secure America's financial independence and colonize
the vast spaces that were presumably already theirs.[7] In the following chapters, I hope to show that American literature, like

American politics and commerce, also saw the transgression of space as a means of achieving revolutionary victory over the European aristocracy.

In chapter 1, I want to identify how the transgression of class operates as an elemental narrative unit in William Godwin's *Caleb Williams*, perhaps the exemplary bourgeois radical novel of eighteenth-century Britain.[8] In chapter 2, I will trace how this narrative is transported to America and adapted to its new environment. In a discussion of Charles Brockden Brown's *Edgar Huntly*, I will examine how certain figural substitutions in the narrative of transgression transform a story about class revolution into a story about foreign expansion. In chapter 3, I will examine how Brown's crude narrative translation is refined and improved by James Fenimore Cooper in an obsessive, relentless body of work which reifies the transgression of space into a system of property ownership and formalizes revolution into a safe place to live. Finally, in chapter 4, I will discuss the regeneration of aristocracy as a sort of annihilative nostalgia in the work of Edgar Allan Poe. Poe borrows the narrative of transgression from both Godwin and Brown, but he never feels comfortable with it. His work describes the anxiety Americans felt the day they realized they had inherited not only a powerful revolutionary propaganda but a vastly brooding slave population which might ask to borrow it sometime.

America never eluded European class politics but rather defined the New World according to already-established political tropes. In so doing, American literature almost systematically erased the distinction between the political world and the natural one. In this conflation, a vast psychological space was born, a space bigger than America itself, one which would remain conceptually inexhaustible long after the entire nation was carpeted with highways and shopping malls. In fact, class politics was never foreign to America but qualified the ways Americans imagined their nation and themselves.

Dreaming
Revolution

1

The Whole Truth

Caleb Williams and the Transgression of Class

The Process of Pursuit

There is a sort of domestic tactics, the object of which is to elude curiosity, and keep up the tenour of conversation, without the disclosure either of our feelings or opinions. The friend of justice will have no object more deeply at heart than the annihilation of this duplicity. . . . It follows that the promoting the best interests of mankind eminently depends upon the freedom of social communication.

—William Godwin, *Enquiry*[1]

By referring to William Godwin's *Things As They Are, or The Adventures of Caleb Williams* as a tale of pursuit, critics have tended to reduce Falkland and Caleb to fixed binary oppositions: oppressor and oppressed, pursuer and pursued, powerful and powerless.[2] Harvey Gross, for example, considers the novel a political allegory of a period when "man was the hunted, the pursued, and society was the hunter, the pursuer."[3] According to this formula, pursuit moves in one direction. It is predicated like a sentence: a coherent, completable act performed upon a discrete, intransitive object.

Such a formula, however, ignores the revolutionary intentions of Godwin's political philosophy. Though *Caleb Williams* describes humankind as the object of tyranny, it simultaneously describes tyranny as the object of reform. It contends that while aristocratic power may limit human freedom, men and women possess the ability to investigate and analyze that power, and, by defining it as illegitimate, to transgress its artificial constraints and bad governments. By penetrating the very skin of coercion, revolutionaries can replace a negative, artificial power (one which limits or represses minds and bodies) with a positive, human authority (one which affirms knowledge, communal relationships, and human consensus). The object of repression describes a scene of revolt that is both political and epistemological.

In Godwin's view, repression compels intellectually curious men and women to investigate their predicament; to this extent, the pursued is often secretly the pursuer. Aristocrats deploy barriers and limits, while intrepid bourgeois investigators analyze every obstacle that stands in their way. Aristocrats shroud their activities in darkness, while commoners peer into every shadow and every crevice, divulging whatever government tries to hide. The aristocrat may possess physical wealth and power, but the reasonable bourgeois revolutionary possesses an inherently human capacity "of perceiving what is eligible and right, of fixing indelibly certain principles upon his mind, and adhering inflexibly to the resolutions he has made" (*Enquiry*, 135). While government pursues individual victims, democratic citizens pursue abstract knowledge and the actual meaning of government.

Even when coerced or imprisoned, Caleb relentlessly uncovers knowledge and explores political secrets. From the beginning he describes himself as "a sort of natural philosopher" and confesses that "the spring of action which, perhaps more than any other,

characterised the whole train of my life, was curiosity. . . . I was
desirous of tracing the variety of effects which might be produced
from given causes."[4] The moment he enters Falkland's home,
Caleb discovers in his new master "an ample field for speculation and conjecture" (6). He questions, investigates, eavesdrops,
discloses; he observes Falkland's solitude, gloom, and gnashing
teeth; he trespasses aristocratic "privacies" and wonders about
padlocked trunks (7). He gathers clues and examines them "a
thousand ways" and from "every point of view" (107). Caleb represents the exemplary Enlightenment philosopher, the sort of
natural scientist who, Ernst Cassirer has argued, believes that humanity, nature, and society are not phenomena "merely to be
looked at, but to be penetrated."[5]

Caleb investigates everything, instinctively seeking to be anywhere he isn't allowed. Since childhood he has been fascinated by
tales of housebreakers, men "to whom locks and bolts were a
jest, and who, vain of their art, exhibited the experiment of
entering a house the most strongly barricaded" (188); ultimately
Caleb even acquires his own mythic reputation as a burglar
trained "in the art of penetrating through walls and doors" (269).
Like Jeremy Bentham's Panopticon, Caleb's gaze penetrates Falkland's conscience, English etymology, secret rooms and gardens,
the "vice and duplicity that must be expected to grow out of injustice" (194), and the lid of the enigmatic trunk which, according to P. N. Furbank, hides "the guilty secret of government."[6]

Caleb never considers himself a free agent, for he recognizes his
allegiance to a greater authority than that of any king. He is
driven by his own "turbulence of curiosity" (143) while drawn
unswervingly to that "omnipotent" truth which is, Godwin explains in his Enquiry, "so far as relates to the conviction of the
understanding, irresistible" (143). For Caleb, as for Bentham, an
ideal society operates according to "a system of inspection, universal, free, and gratuitous, the most effectual and permanent of
all securities against abuse."[7]

Because truth is irresistible, Caleb uncovers his master's guilt
without requiring Falkland's eventual confession or any material
evidence whatsoever. He simply determines to watch Falkland
"without remission" in order to "trace all the mazes of his
thought" (126). Caleb decides that since Falkland is a member
of the human community whether he likes it or not, he cannot
hide his feelings; ultimately "his secret anguish must betray it-

self" (126). When Caleb takes his place in the courtroom over which Falkland ironically presides, he brings with him a system of justice that judges and lawyers don't normally recognize. Caleb takes his seat and Falkland notices him instantly. As Caleb describes:

> It happened in this, as in some preceding instances; we exchanged a silent look by which we told volumes to each other. Mr. Falkland's expression turned from red to pale, and from pale to red. I perfectly understood his feelings, and would willingly have withdrawn myself. But it was impossible; my passions were too deeply engaged; I was rooted to the spot; though my own life, that of my master, or almost of a whole nation had been at stake, I had no power to change my position. (126)

Caleb feels gripped by a form of passion which Godwin characterizes as "the ardour and vehemence of mind with which any object is pursued" (Enquiry, 136). It is a passion more powerful than people or nations, irresistibly transporting Caleb to a realm of perfect reason where all material and social distinctions are leveled by the all-comprehending gaze of omnipotent truth. Here the identities of pursuer and pursued, judge and defendant, master and servant are joined indissolubly together. When Caleb and Falkland's eyes meet, they silently confess "volumes" to one another. They do not choose to read one another; they simply must.

While Falkland's courtroom grinds out its mockery of justice, truth reveals itself to Caleb's intimate thoughts, implicating him in a system of judgment at once private and irrefutable. By gazing into one another's eyes, Caleb and Falkland share everything: Falkland's guilt, Caleb's recognition, and the secret complicity of government. Unable to "endure" Caleb's penetration, Falkland rushes out of the courtroom; and while Caleb drifts off deeper into his own introspection, his judgment of Falkland grows more powerful and convincing—if only to himself. He describes the verdict gathering in him as "involuntary" (129); he doesn't pronounce judgment against Falkland so much as act as the medium through which immanent reason speaks. As he exits the courtroom, he hears the voice of justice arise inside his own heart:

> I hastened into the garden, and plunged into the deepest of its thickets. My mind was full almost to bursting. I no sooner

conceived myself sufficiently removed from all observation,
than my thoughts forced their way spontaneously to my
tongue, and I exclaimed in a fit of uncontrollable enthusiasm:
"This is the murderer! the Hawkinses were innocent! I am sure
of it! I will pledge my life for it! It is out! It is discovered!
Guilty upon my soul!" (129)

Surrounded by the "thickets" of nature, invisible to the observations of government, Caleb speaks his irresistible judgment of
Falkland like a sort of "uncontrollable" spasm. He doesn't grasp
truth; he is gripped by it. In Godwin's metaphysic, individuals
don't govern, only truth does. By surrendering to immanent reason, Caleb feels "as if my animal system had undergone a total
revolution. . . . I was never so perfectly alive as at that moment" (129–130). By transgressing Falkland's privileged reputation, Caleb undergoes both a physical and a moral transforma-
tion; by seeing through Falkland, Caleb implicates himself in the
vaster revolution of universes and the more intimate revolutions
of bodies. According to Godwin, truth compels honest people and
forces them to see through the duplicities and deceptions upon
which false governments are founded. It is a truth which breaks
through the superficial constraints and coercions of government
by driving people with its own irresistible conviction. It does not
seek to coerce citizens but to *be* them, investing discrete individuals with common, indivisible reason. Truth and reason replace
the self-interest of individuals, investing them with a democratic
force equal to nature and more powerful than government.[8]

The Pursuer, Pursued

Just as the victim ultimately vanquishes, the pursuer ultimately surrenders.

Falkland's murder of Tyrrel is savage and spontaneous, lacking
the customary refinements of a duel. "I watched my opportunity," he confesses to Caleb, "followed Mr. Tyrrel from the rooms,
seized a sharp-pointed knife that fell in my way, came behind
him, and stabbed him to the heart" (135). Falkland fears that
public knowledge of his crime will strip him of his "mysterious
sort of divinity annexed to the person of a true knight" (97). If
an ability to penetrate surfaces describes Caleb's authority, then

an ability to remain impenetrable behind the walls of reputation describes Falkland's power. Falkland considers his reputation a "divinity" which, long after he dies, will see that his "fame shall still survive" (282). So long as Falkland can keep himself closed up inside his reputation like a knight in brassy armor, his power will seem "insurmountable" and sufficient to grind Caleb "into atoms" (284).[9]

Rudolf F. Storch is wrong to suggest that Falkland's relentless persecution of Caleb "cannot be explained rationally," nor does Falkland simply "enjoy terrorizing his victims."[10] Politically, at least, his motives make perfect sense. Caleb's discoveries threaten to disrupt not only Falkland's reputation but the very system of power which helps him maintain it. Falkland depends on strategic inequalities: class, money, name, and position. If he is reduced to equality with men like Caleb, he loses everything. Falkland is as much a prisoner of his social position as Caleb is later the prisoner of stone walls. Falkland cannot socialize freely with other men or they will learn how much like them he really is.

True to his nature, Falkland is fundamentally a man of reason, and, as a result, is deeply aware of his own hypocrisy. As he tells Caleb during his confession:

> "This it is to be a gentleman! a man of honour! I was the fool
> of fame. My virtue, my honesty, my everlasting peace of mind
> were cheap sacrifices to be made at the shrine of this divinity.
> But, what is worse, there is nothing that has happened that
> has in any degree contributed to my cure. I am as much the
> fool of fame as ever. I cling to it to my last breath. Though I
> be the blackest of villains, I will leave behind me a spotless
> and illustrious name. There is no crime so malignant, no
> scene of blood so horrible, in which that object cannot engage
> me." (135–136)

Falkland recognizes evil as something exterior to his true nature, a mask which has gained mastery over the man. Falkland is both victim and victimizer, just and unjust, reasonable man and unreasoning tyrant. Because of Falkland's dual character, Caleb's feelings for him alternate between reverence and hatred. He reveres the authentic divinity of Falkland's human soul but despises the false divinity of Falkland's "illustrious name."

In order to preserve his reputation, Falkland drives himself into seclusion and away from the "busy haunts of men" (6). When

Caleb's curiosity continues to advance, Falkland begins to "live in perpetual fear" of Caleb's "penetration" (136). He abandons his few remaining friends and even the remonstrances of his own guilty conscience, wandering off to lie "for whole nights together under the naked cope of heaven," finding in the stars "that uproar of the elements which partially called off his attention from the discord and dejection which occupied his own mind" (124). Where Caleb seeks to understand both scientific causes and human essences, Falkland prefers to flee both. Fearing exposure, the aristocrat buries his democratic nature so deeply that even his benevolence becomes "veiled and concealed" (139). Falkland is terrified that the revelation of his crimes (like the previous revelation of Tyrrel's) will "so irresistibly address themselves to the indignation of mankind, that, like death, they [will] level all distinctions, and reduce their perpetrator to an equality with the most indigent and squalid of his species" (92). By concealing his guilt, Falkland surrenders himself to the same fate he predicted for Tyrrel: "If you would not hear the universal indignation of mankind, you must not come into the society of men" (95).

Falkland's confession to Caleb is illegitimate because it is made under "every seal of secrecy" (136). He refuses to surrender himself to truth; he doesn't believe that facts should be freely disseminated according to public will but only deployed according to private interest. Truth, he explains, is not "entitled to adoration for its own sake" but rather "for the sake of the happiness it is calculated to produce" (282). To this extent, Falkland doesn't see truth as a condition of life but as a strategy of politics. Truth is something Falkland uses to his own purposes and to maintain his own authority; he considers himself truth's master and the architect of his own redemption. He claims he has atoned for his murder of Tyrrel, as well as his consequent complicity in the execution of the unfortunate Hawkinses, because his subsequent life "has all been spent in acts of benevolence" (281). Like the hypothetical aristocrat Godwin complains about in his *Enquiry*, Falkland mistakenly assumes that "it is the business of a wise man not to subvert, either in himself or others, delusions which are useful, and prejudices which are salutary" (296). For Falkland, reason is not democratic but class-interested; aristocratic duplicity is necessary and ultimately beneficial in the scheme of "things as they are." The nobility must determine what sort of knowledge the ignoble masses deserve.[11]

The Secret Life of Repression

In his *Enquiry*, Godwin argues that a truly virtuous society is built upon a foundation of natural laws, not human contracts, for

> every conceivable mode of action has its appropriate tendency, and shade of tendency, to benefit, or to mischief, and consequently its appropriate claim to be performed or avoided. Thus clearly does it appear that promises and compacts are not the foundation of morality. . . . Secondly, I observe that promises are, absolutely considered, an evil, and stand in opposition to the genuine and wholesome exercise of an intellectual nature. (218)

According to Godwin, a pact between individuals excludes the common interests of all humanity. By agreeing to Falkland's secret pact, Caleb doesn't simply subject himself to the prison of government but discounts the interests of humanity-at-large by working against a system of free and unimpeded social communication. When Falkland dictates the oath of allegiance, Caleb repeats it "with an aching heart. I had no power to offer a word of remark" (135). Again Caleb feels transfixed, but this time it is by untruth and the deceptions of government. By agreeing to protect Falkland's reputation, Caleb agrees to protect the system of his own persecution. By betraying humankind's interests, he must, like Falkland, abandon the society of free-speaking individuals.

From the moment he signs his contract with Falkland, Caleb recalls:

> I was tormented with a secret of which I must never disburthen myself; and this consciousness was at my age a source of perpetual melancholy. I had made myself a prisoner, in the most intolerable sense of that term, for years, perhaps for the rest of my life. Though my prudence and discretion should be invariable, I must remember that I should have an overseer, vigilant from conscious guilt, full of resentment at the unjustifiable means by which I had extorted from him a confession. (138)

Like Falkland, Caleb agrees to enforce the conspiracy of government and must withdraw from the public eye as a result. He terminates his frank conversations with Forester and grows moody and iconoclastic, compromising his essential virtue—that virtue

which, Godwin explains in his *Enquiry*, "is inseparably connected with knowledge" (301).

Caleb never escapes Falkland's "lynx-eyed jealousy" (146) because he has voluntarily submitted to Falkland's dishonest government. "Estrangement from human society," he learns from experience, is like an "eternal penance" (143) because it divides his
individual spirit from the company of all people, burdening him
with a sense of aloneness he must carry into every community he
enters. Even when Forester's letter lures Caleb home to plead his
case in open court, Caleb mistakenly assumes he will be allowed
to contend with Falkland's accusations "in the light of day," but
by refusing to confess what he knows about Falkland, he casts
doubts upon his testimony and character; it becomes immediately apparent to the court, and even to Caleb's strongest advo-
cate, Forester, that he is hiding something. Foolishly Caleb has
imagined that he can affirm his honesty while refusing to speak
the whole truth. "You are a man of penetration," he tells Forester;
"look at me, do you see any of the marks of guilt?" (171). But
Forester, like the courtroom over which he presides, is concerned
with appearances rather than truth, and Caleb has made the "appearances" of his case begin to look implausible by refusing to
confess everything he knows.[12]

Even when Caleb escapes the "secrets of a prison," he can't so
easily escape the secrets of his own repression (180). Like his fictional successor Vautrin, Caleb is a master of disguise and a con-
summate mimic. But every attempt at self-concealment makes
Caleb prey to the men who are employed by secret governments,
men of "strict honour" such as Gines (260). A private detective
hired by Falkland, Gines initially locates Caleb after hearing him
described as "a person who did every thing by proxy, and made a
secret of all his motions" (264). And by hiding his true character,
Caleb estranges himself from the sympathetic people who want
to protect him: Mr. Spurrel betrays Caleb not because he knows
who Caleb really is but because he believes he is who he pretends
to be, and Laura Denison deserts him because, like Forester, she
instinctively realizes he is lying to her (300). Caleb aids his un-
virtuous pursuers by compromising his own inherent virtue. Before Caleb can exonerate his name, he must recognize the futility
of any type of duplicity, even his own.[13] Ultimately he decides:
"There was one expedient against which I was absolutely deter-

mined, disguise. I had experienced so many mortifications and such intolerable restraint when I formerly had recourse to it, it was associated in my memory with sensations of such acute anguish, that my mind was thus far entirely convinced: Life was not worth purchasing at so high a price!" (305).

Rexford Stamper incorrectly suggests that Caleb is not a tragic character because his punishment is not the result of "his violation of an external code of conduct."[14] In fact, Caleb has violated the most rigorous standard of Godwinian virtue: he has aided government by establishing zones of concealment and elision. He has drawn a curtain across the secrets of his own heart, mistaking individual self-interest for the greater interests of all "Mankind." In order to exonerate his name, he must reach beyond the confines of himself to discover a more universal system of government. In order to save himself, he must first learn that he alone is not worth saving.

The Subversion of the Subject

Let us consider the effect that coercion produces upon the mind of him against whom it is employed. It cannot begin with convincing; it is no argument. It begins with producing the sensation of pain, and the sentiment of distaste. It begins with violently alienating the mind from the truth with which we wish it to be impressed. It includes in it a tacit confession of imbecility. If he who employs coercion against me could mould me to his purposes by argument, no doubt he would. He pretends to punish me because his argument is strong; but he really punishes me because his argument is weak.

—William Godwin, *Enquiry*

In their penultimate confrontation, Falkland presents Caleb with a document. By signing it, Caleb will effectively deny any knowledge of Falkland's crimes. The document represents a paradigmatic social contract, an individual's primal act of Rousseauist Original Sin: the surrender of one's natural state of reason, knowledge, and virtue to the governmental trinity of fear, honor, and coercion. Caleb refuses to sign Falkland's compact because he has learned that Falkland's power over him is utterly counterfeit.

Falkland's attempts to convince Caleb that his power is insur-   *11*
mountable are contradicted by his increasingly "death-like" and   *The*
"more than mortal" appearance (284). Caleb begins to wonder: *Whole*
If Falkland is as powerful as he claims, why does he demand that   *Truth*
Caleb sign a document legally protecting him? If Falkland is truly
unbeatable, why must he profess it so loudly? As a result of these
reflections, Caleb begins "to imagine that all I had heard from
this dreadful adversary was mere madness and extravagance, that
he was at length deprived of the use of reason, which had long
served him only as a medium of torment" (285).

Caleb ultimately realizes that Falkland is not granted power by
his class position but by Caleb's mistaken respect for that position. Caleb has sanctioned the false divinity of Falkland's reputation by disregarding that, in Godwin's words,

> one of the most essential ingredients in a virtuous character is
> undaunted firmness; and nothing can more powerfully tend to
> destroy this principle than the spirit of a monarchical govern-
> ment. The first lesson of virtue is, Fear no man; the first lesson
> of such a constitution is, Fear the king. The true interest of
> man requires the annihilation of factitious and imaginary dis-
> tinctions; it is inseparable from monarchy to support and ren-
> der them more palpable than ever. He that cannot speak to
> the proudest despot with a consciousness that he is a man
> speaking to a man, and a determination to yield him no supe-
> riority to which his inherent qualifications do not entitle him,
> is wholly incapable of an illustrious virtue. (*Enquiry*, 445)

The king does not rule but rather his subjects submit. Even physical coercion is not imposed upon democratic citizens so much as
permitted by them. Individuals must see through the "imaginary distinctions" created by monarchical institutions; they must
speak to everybody and not submit to anybody.

Caleb ultimately learns that revolutionaries do not need to ex-
ert physical force to achieve successful revolutions. Instead, they
merely need to utter the truth with their tongues, enunciating
that primal authority before which "Tyrants have trembled surrounded with whole armies of their Janissaries!" Nothing can
make Falkland "inaccessible" to his fury, Caleb tells him, for
true revolutionaries do not require "daggers" with which to slay
their oppressors but only the ability to "unfold a tale" (314). For
Godwin, revolutionaries subvert governments with their innate

ability to speak the truth; by pronouncing a language of transgressive signification, they overleap the appearances manufactured by governments. Citizens do not have to live within the artificial limits of government because they can speak *through* those limits; the language of common individuals can make words true again and people equal. The simple utterance of truth is itself a sort of political revolt, for "imperfect institutions . . . cannot long support themselves, when they are generally disapproved of, and their effects truly understood. . . . [T]hey may be expected to decline and expire, almost without any effort" (*Enquiry*, 243).

Caleb Williams's thematic unity has been challenged in recent years, particularly since D. Gilbert Dumas recovered Godwin's original ending (this ending describes Caleb reimprisoned and Falkland's reputation triumphant—though Falkland himself apparently dies of guilt). In both the original and published versions, however, the fates of Caleb and Falkland are made deliberately ambiguous, conflating the identities of pursuer and pursued, hero and villain. When Dumas claims that "the narrative's implicit argument moves from a political generalization . . . to an ethical one," he mistakenly assumes these are two separate issues.[15] But as Mitzi Meyers explains, for Godwin all "political problems are essentially moral problems."[16]

Godwin transgresses political reality in order to establish transcendent moral imperatives. In both versions of the ending, Caleb journeys beyond the political and legal dimensions of Falkland's crime to recognize his own complicity in the vaster crimes of society. Citizens allow the corruptions of government to persist because they refuse to hear the wisdom of their own hearts. Godwin's revised ending emphasizes that people have neglected their natural duties and allowed individuals like Falkland to happen. Ideally, society should help Falkland become the better man he secretly knows himself to be and teach him his responsibilities to the greater community. Instead, it punishes Falkland for being the man it has made him.

In Godwin's revised ending, Caleb decides that in order to transgress government he must first transgress the limits of his own individuality. By driving through the limits of everything he is, he can realize the entirety of everything humanity has ever been and ever could be. Caleb finally asks himself, "Why should my reflections perpetually centre upon myself? self, an overweening regard to which has been the source of my errors! Falkland, I will think only of thee, and from that thought will draw ever fresh nourishment for my sorrows! One generous, one disinterested tear I will consecrate to thy ashes! A nobler spirit lived not among the sons of men" (325). By regaining transcendent reason and classlessness, Caleb and Falkland meet again in the place they have met before: the realm of perfect, indivisible Truth. By reaching beyond the confines of "self," Caleb and Falkland acquire a more limitless and universal property: the metaphysical planet of Mankind. "I began these memoirs with the idea of vindicating my character," Caleb concludes. "I have now no character that I wish to vindicate" (326). In the arena of the courts, real individuals are never recognized; in the vaster universe of truth, they don't need to be.

When Caleb and Falkland last meet in a courtroom, real justice is achieved in the gaze they share between them, the multiperspective "eye of power" which is at once intimate, private, impersonal, and boundless.[17] By honestly telling his story, Caleb absorbs and sublimates Falkland's righteous indignation in their common sympathy. As Caleb observes:

> he could no longer resist. He saw my sincerity; he was penetrated with my grief and compunction. He rose from his seat supported by the attendants, and—to my infinite astonishment—threw himself into my arms!
>
> "Williams," said he, "you have conquered!" (324)

By conquering Falkland, Caleb reduces both pursuer and pursued to brothers in arms; they regain their "magnetical sympathy" in a realm of truth where all distinctions (even those of individual character and personality) are leveled. The "conquest" of aristocrats does not designate them as Other but embraces them as Same. They transgress the power of government in order to submit to the more irrefutable authority of themselves.

2

The Great Sea-Change

Edgar Huntly and the Transgression of Space

The Cause of America

*The cause of America is in a great
measure the cause of all mankind. Many
circumstances hath, and will arise, which are
not local, but universal, and through which
the principles of all Lovers of Mankind are
affected, and in the Event of which, their
Affections are interested. The laying a
Country desolate with Fire and Sword,
declaring War against the natural rights of
all Mankind, and extirpating the Defenders
thereof from the Face of the Earth, is the
concern of every Man to whom Nature hath
given the Power of feeling.*

—Tom Paine, *Common Sense*[1]

Just as Godwin elevated class conflict to the status of epistemology, Tom Paine, one of *Political Justice*'s earliest admirers,
transformed America's revolt against England into a sort of geopolitical anthropology. For Paine, the American Revolution never
simply represented an individual nation of people disputing a set
of royal prerogatives; it tried to establish worldwide principles of
self-government in the "cause of all mankind." Ultimately the
"Power of feeling" that all people shared would open up the political disputes of specific colonial territories to a more universal
system of justice and human administration.[2]

According to Paine, America revolted not only against another
nation or another class but against the rude presumptions of European maps. In the same way that Falkland confined Caleb with
prisons and bad laws, England confined the free spirit of Americans by imposing self-interested trade routes and artificial borders. Where Caleb's triumph over Falkland is validated by a dream
of regaining natural justice, America's dispute with England is
validated by the dream of a return to natural space. As Paine
argues in *Common Sense*:

> Europe is too thickly planted with kingdoms to be long at
> peace, and whenever a war breaks out between England and
> any foreign power, the trade of America goes to ruin, *because
> of her connection with Britain.* The next war may not turn
> out like the last, and should it not, the advocates for recon-
> ciliation now, will be wishing for separation then, because,
> neutrality in that case, would be a safer convoy than a man of
> war. Every thing that is right or natural pleads for separation.
> The blood of the slain, the weeping voice of nature cries, 'TIS
> TIME TO PART. Even the distance at which the Almighty
> hath placed England and America, is a strong and natural
> proof, that the authority of the one, over the other, was never
> the design of Heaven. (40–41)

Paine claims American businesses are suffering because international politics hasn't learned the lesson of colonial geography.
America must politically separate itself from England because it
is already physically separate and because the deployment of continents reminds tyrants of the integrity of nations. When people
"separate" themselves from systems of traditional authority, they
assert not only independence but the manifest "design of Heaven."
True authority only emerges from a nation divided from its gov-

ernments; by creating this division spatially, citizens assert the
independence of their hearts.

While Britain justifies its excessive taxation by claiming to protect colonial citizens from French trade incursions, Paine argues
that recent hostilities have resulted from European political divisions, not transatlantic ones. Men fight when their nations
are artificially crowded too close together, not when they are
spread evenly across the always-abundant natural world. By step-
ping west into the outlaw frontier, settlers create new spaces
of prosperity and peace. Nature's "weeping voice" cries out for
Americans to transgress British trade routes in order to reclaim
their natural rights to a free and unimpeded international commerce. Americans must transgress British laws in order to reclaim
their inalienable human rights. They must abandon Europe in
order to become independent citizens of the world.

When Americans subvert international space, they assert political order; and when they subvert political laws, they draw a
more democratic map. The lesson of geography is ultimately a
revolutionary one. It is "absurd," Paine argues, for anyone to ex-
pect "a continent to be perpetually governed by an island. In no
instance hath nature made the satellite larger than its primary
planet, and as England and America, with respect to each other,
reverses the common order of nature, it is evident they belong to
different systems; England to Europe, America to itself" (43).
Paine's revolution reaches across space the same way Godwin's
reaches across class. In America, revolutionaries aren't supposed
to penetrate other classes; they are supposed to penetrate political
landscapes. While England belongs to a system of European nations, America belongs only to itself, bound together by the common sympathies of its citizens.[3] The English struggle against other
people and countries to assert dominion, economy, and independence; Americans, however, assert their national will by exploring the manifest shape and destiny of their so far undiscovered
continent. While England belongs to a differentiated government
of hierarchical classes and races, America belongs to the undifferentiated "common order of nature." At a time when English lib-
erals like Godwin are exploring the nature of Mankind, Americans are divulging the landscape of a nation.

American notions of revolution worked to shape a weirdly dis-
sonant type of domestic imagination. For Americans, revolution
did not describe the confrontation of two classes but rather the

displacement of one class by another. Middle-class Americans asserted their natural rights to democratic freedom by moving *away* from the scene of dispute. It was a conflict waged through a strategy of misdirection. Instead of trying to break through the dark injustice of aristocratic properties and institutions, commoners were supposed to move into the wilderness, where they would establish better laws, nations, and governments. Americans like Paine weren't simply trying to redefine the notion of class but the physical body and *difference* of an entire country. Democrats did not define their political difference and integrity by opposing aristocratic demesnes but by vanishing into places they had never been.

As Eric Foner explains, Paine's "conviction that America was marked by economic abundance and an approximate equality of condition prevented him from carrying republican egalitarianism to its radical anti-aristocratic extreme."[4] The very existence of America, like the existence of Godwin's ideal "natural man," made human conditions equal because it provided a ground of infinite and abundant possibilities. By defining equality in terms of geography rather than class, Paine and other revolutionaries elided the fundamental class nature of American independence.[5] Instead of taking their property from rulers and nobles, Americans imagined they were taking it from the boundless resources of nature. They did not cross the fences of aristocratic estates but rather the perpetually receding border of the American frontier. As a result, American revolutionaries often disregarded the very issues of class which originally struck their nation into existence. It became common, in fact, for politicians like Melancton Smith to assert, as in the Constitutional Debates of 1788, that in America class was never a significant political issue, since "it is our singular felicity that we have no legal or hereditary distinctions of this kind."[6]

The Object of Reading

How barren and limited must be the capacity of that man who can be instructed or delighted only in contemplating the ideas of others. When you read, your books ought to be considered as a text to which your imagination must furnish a supplement and commentary. The ideas of others are to

*you of no importance and utility but as you render them by
meditation your own and make them as the soil or stock,
which, with proper culture, may be productive of numberless
others, the products of your own labor, or the offspring of your
own imagination.*

*There is no sphere, however limited, in which human nature
may not sufficiently be studied, and in which sufficient
opportunities are not afforded for the exercise of the deepest
penetration, and as a philosopher is able [to] derive
amusement [and] instruction from contemplating a post or
stone, so he whose descriptive powers are vigorous can
always make the delineation of them a source of pleasure and
improvement. The book of nature, like every other volume,
is useful to the reader exactly in proportion to his sagacity
and to the attention with which he pursues it, but what
advantages can he derive from it, whose rapid and unsteady
glances can produce none but general and indeterminate
ideas, who dwells not on a single object long enough to know
its properties?*

—Charles Brockden Brown,
    letter to Henrietta G.[7]

Reading, Charles Brockden Brown suggests, is like the study of
nature. It colonizes texts and makes them productive, investing
them with imagination and labor. Just as readers transgress the
literal meaning of words in books in order to cultivate the excessive gardens of their own imaginations, philosophers transgress
limits of the "known" in order to reap "advantages" from the unknown and develop wider "properties." Both writing and philosophy help to establish ownership over nature's abundance. Both
texts and appearances can be penetrated just as the wilderness
can be colonized, thus yielding a limitless field of surplus which,
when trained "with proper culture," will produce more surplus
to reinvest, more possibilities to reconsider, and more spaces to
wonder at.

American colonialism was driven by the assumption that
transgressing nature established a sort of geopolitical integrity.
By describing its work as "reaping" and "sowing," colonialism
naturalized itself as part of the seasonal cycle, just as capitalism
naturalized itself by pretending to adhere to the "natural" laws of

a purportedly "free market." The limitless surplus, or what Brown refers to as the "supplement," is produced by physical and imaginative labor. In other words, people make nature limitless by exploiting it. By working nature with their minds and their tools, they make nature productive the same way they make books meaningful—by investing them with human ideas, human perfectibility, human potential, and human ambition. The colonial mind envisions the wilderness as a field of infinite exploitation, an invitation to unlimited conjecture. To both the pioneer and the novelist, America stood for what R. W. B. Lewis calls "space as spaciousness, as the unbounded, the area of total possibility."[8] America didn't simply represent a map of what was; it marked the space of everything that could be.

In *Love and Death and the American Novel*, Leslie A. Fiedler claims that literary genres are never transported to the New World intact like so many canned vegetables but suffer in their journey a set of profound cultural transformations. Speaking about the European gothic, Fiedler claims that the transportation of a genre

> *involves a profound change of meaning*. In the American gothic, that is to say, the heathen, unredeemed wilderness and not the decaying monuments of a dying class, nature and not society becomes the symbol of evil. Similarly not the aristocrat but the Indian, not the dandified courtier but the savage colored man is postulated as the embodiment of villainy. Our novel of terror, that is to say (even before its founder has consciously shifted his political allegiances), is well on the way to becoming a Calvinist exposé of natural human corruption rather than an enlightened attack on a debased ruling class or entrenched superstition.[9]

Fiedler assumes that colonial literature depoliticizes (and thus "humanizes") literary tradition. The "change of meaning" described by American literature marks a "shift of political allegiances," one which is no longer concerned with how class systems operate so much as how human beings behave. The American metaphysics of self drains the novel of its European political content while preserving the rudimentary "form" of the European gothic, recoding its protagonists and remapping its landscapes. Like many of the American writers he discusses, Fiedler believes that old narrative forms, applied to the American continent, produce new types of knowledge and new ranges of meaning. American literature is "naive" because it rejects the hard, literal ingredients of class, economy, and politics. It does not speak the known so much as resound with intimations of the unknowable. It is not literal but inexplicable; not representative but symbolic.[10] Like many of his fellow postwar Americanists (Matthieson, Chase, Fiedelson, Jr., and even Leo Marx), Fiedler believes that American literature applies old narrative forms to the wider visions of a more indefinite country, discarding the dull facts of history while engendering old genres with new complexity. While individuals transgress the world of experience to make both themselves and the world more productive, novelists transgress novelistic form in order to produce greater and richer systems of meaning.

In his preface to *Edgar Huntly; or Memoirs of a Sleep-Walker*, Charles Brockden Brown, like Fiedler, suggests that Americans can apply European genres to the new land and make it more productive. As Brown explains:

> America has opened new views to the naturalist and politician, but has seldom furnished themes to the moral painter. That new springs of action, and new motives to curiosity should operate; that the field of investigation, opened to us by our own country, should differ essentially from those which exist in Europe, may be readily conceived. . . .
>
> One merit the writer may at least claim; that of calling forth the passions and engaging the sympathy of the reader, by means hitherto unemployed by preceding authors. Puerile superstitions and exploded manners; Gothic castles and chimeras, are the materials usually employed for this end. The incidents of Indian hostility, and the perils of the Western wilderness, are far more suitable; and, for a native of America to overlook these, would admit of no apology.[11]

According to Brown, authors cultivate American landscapes the same way pioneers colonize the wilderness. Novelists apply European genres to American landscapes the same way colonists apply European tools to the soil or European Bibles to aboriginal inhabitants. The process of production does not change, only its "field of investigation." The American novelist does not create new stories but substitutes American elements for European ones. American gothic invokes the same readerly "passions" and "sympathy" as the traditional European gothic, but by substituting entirely new "means" and "materials." As Fiedler observes, American gothic replaces the figure of the castle with the figure of the wilderness, the power-mad aristocrat with the utterly savage Indian, but Fiedler is wrong to contend that these substitutions create narratives which are less "political" or more "natural" than before. For colonial writers such as Brown, the westward movement into space resounds with political implications. By substituting "nature" for "government," American writers naturalize imperialist ideology by resorting to the same narrative structure Godwin and other Enlightenment radicals had used to naturalize class revolution. Americans never abandoned the narrative of transgression so much as redeployed it.[12]

Edgar Huntly *and the Boundaries of Class*

Like Caleb Williams, Edgar Huntly considers curiosity "its own reward. Knowledge is of value for its own sake, and pleasure is annexed to the acquisition, without regard to any thing beyond" (16). Edgar characteristically wants to disclose the secrets hidden behind false appearances; he wants to cross the border of what *seems* to explore the reality of what *is*. Both Caleb and Edgar are inspired by the unknown and unsolved; they seek to divulge spaces which are at once psychological and geographic. But while Caleb explores aristocratic estates and courtrooms, Edgar explores the unmapped wilderness; where Caleb pours over public documents, Edgar pours over "the brooks . . . the pits and hollows, that were adjacent to the scene of blood" (8). While Falkland retreats behind the walls of his formidable reputation, Clithero flees into places "obscured by the melancholy umbrage of pines, whose eternal murmurs are in unison with vacancy and solitude" (96).

Clithero's "pensive and reserved deportment" arouses Edgar's natural curiosity. Like Caleb, Edgar believes he must simply observe his quarry without remission if he wants to reveal Clithero's guilt. As Edgar explains, "Henceforth this man was to become the subject of my scrutiny. I was to gain all the knowledge, respecting him, which those with whom he lived, and were the perpetual witnesses of his actions, could impart. For this end I was to make minute inquiries, and to put seasonable interrogatories. From this conduct I promised myself an ultimate solution of my doubts" (15).

Charles Brockden Brown was not simply influenced by Godwin's political philosophy, he was obsessed by Godwin's greatest novel.[13] To some extent, each of Brown's four major novels attempts to transfer *Caleb Williams* to a colonial setting, but with the possible exception of *Arthur Mervyn*, Brown never follows Godwin's outline more meticulously than in his hasty captivity-narrative pastiche, *Edgar Huntly*.[14] Like *Caleb Williams*, *Edgar Huntly* is the tale of a murder and its investigation. Its protagonist is middle class, self-consciously rational, and remorseless in his pursuit of the truth. Like Caleb, Edgar believes he can solve the crime of Waldegrave's murder by simply examining the first person to arouse his suspicions. And like *Caleb Williams*, *Edgar Huntly* is divided into two distinct pursuit narratives. In the first, the protagonist is confronted with an unsolved crime, as well as a male suspect of impenetrable character. In the second, the protagonist's investigation of his suspect leads him across spaces that extend both horizontally and vertically. The following narrative oppositions describe the transatlantic shift from class to nature as the metaphoric object of pursuit:

Falkland	Aristocracy/government
Caleb	Bourgeois individualism
Clithero	Wilderness/Indians
Edgar	American colonialism

In *Edgar Huntly*, however, the mystery never yields a simple solution, and the impenetrable suspect never betrays his true character. In fact, like all of Brown's novels, *Edgar Huntly* takes a long time getting nowhere; there is something infinitely regressive about Brown's plots which is both psychologically disturbing and narratively unsatisfying. A reader does not progress through Brown's novels so much as become mired in their expanding atmosphere of paranoia and indeterminacy. While Caleb eventually sees through Falkland and finds his way back to society, Edgar never really solves anything or gets anywhere—at least not through his own conscious volition. In fact, Edgar rarely knows where he is or what he is doing, and by the time he returns home again he has already begun to subside into what Norman S.

Grabo refers to as the conclusion's "curious inconclusiveness."[15]
But while Edgar never divulges irrefutable truths or a system of
benign epistemology at the heart of human nature, he does struggle to live the same *story* as Caleb, or at least wanders through
the same motions in a sort of somnambulistic drowse.

Edgar's search for Waldegrave's murderer leads him away from
any practical solution to the crime. Like Caleb, he uncovers the
secrets of men, but unlike him he never completely understands
what those secrets mean. Early in his story Edgar cries out in
wonder at how "sudden and enormous" is "the transition from
uncertainty to knowledge!" (6). But as readers proceed through
Brown's circuitous maze of false clues and postponed revelations,
they only learn that every narrative "transition," so far as Brown
is concerned, is itself terribly uncertain. Edgar never really learns
anything substantial so much as he realizes how complicated and
inconclusive knowing can be. Attempting to solve the murder of
his friend Waldegrave, Edgar convinces Clithero, a sleepwalking
Irish immigrant, to confess his crimes, and as a result he hears a
story which has nothing to do with Waldegrave whatsoever. By
pursuing Clithero into the wilderness, Edgar uncovers a conspiracy of Indians who want to murder him, as they have already
murdered other members of his family. Every narrative gambit
leads Edgar not to any believable resolution but to yet another eccentric diversion. There are times when Brown seems to be search-
ing for Waldegrave's murderer as frantically as Edgar himself.

Every secret opens onto another secret, like a diminishing se-
quence of Chinese puzzle boxes.[16] For Brown, and for American
storytellers in general, the wilderness never divulges the location
of ultimate truth so much as a motive for perpetual progress.
Americans never discover the final ground of the westward movement but only provisional base camps along the way to a constantly postponed denouement. Imperialism doesn't want to establish a final frontier and then return home to its beginning; it
wants to establish an infinite series of places from which it can
always begin again. It doesn't want to return home so much as
take home with it.

In order to "Americanize" *Caleb Williams*, Brown must seal
the ideological break between its two narratives. Since Falkland's
"reputation" signifies the superficiality of both aristocratic personality and public government, the psychological and political
narratives for Godwin are perfectly continuous. In order to under-

stand how bad governments oppress good citizens, Godwin needs

to explain how good citizens can oppress both themselves and
one another with bad ideas. In America, however, people don't
learn to build better governments by revealing their true selves;
instead, they build a better nation by journeying into the wilderness and making it safe for democracy. They make their nation
stronger by discovering more room for their nation to occupy.

Edgar's "minute" study of Clithero never divulges immutable
truths but only perpetual "obscurities" and "obstacles" (23).
Where Caleb eventually learns the truth about Falkland's secret
thoughts and government's oppressive conspiracies, Edgar uncovers only vacancies, lapses, and discontinuities, a constant deferral
or postponement of narrative resolution. From the beginning, Edgar identifies the secret convolutions of Clithero's mind with his
"trackless and intricate" journeys into the woods at night (9).
While Caleb finally discloses the contents of Falkland's padlocked
trunk, Edgar never discovers anything pertinent at the "hundred
times examined" trunk of the elm where Waldegrave was murdered (8). When Edgar glimpses the sleepwalking Clithero two
nights in a row, he never confronts him as he originally intended
or tries to wake him to the reality of his actions; instead, Edgar
allows himself to be led away from the scene of the crime and
into the "trackless" woods. Clithero's route is "a maze, oblique,
circuitous, upward and downward," managing to "bewilder or
fatigue his pursuer" at the same time it testifies to Clithero's intrepid colonial spirit (23). Even in his sleep Clithero seeks to
"pierce into the deepest thickets, to plunge into the darkest cavi-
ties, to ascend the most difficult heights, and approach the slippery and tremulous verge of the dizziest precipices" (23). Rather
than uncover humanity's common reason, Edgar discovers in
Clithero the relentless hunger of imperial expansion—the irresistible drive into any and all territories that have yet to be known,
the ceaselessly unconscious pursuit of the "deepest," the "darkest,"
the "most difficult heights," and the "dizziest precipices" (23).

What Edgar ultimately learns from his pursuit of Clithero is the
fact of his own "roaming disposition," as well as his own innate
desire to transgress the wilderness's most unreachable spaces
(97). The further Clithero leads Edgar from civilization, the more
Edgar desires to exceed Clithero's relentless adventuring. Even
though Edgar has always loved to "immerse" himself "in shades
and dells, and hold converse with the solemnities and secrecies

of nature," Clithero's disappearances inspire him to discover shad-
ier and more secret places than he has known before; Clithero's
disappearances provide him "new incitements" to climb nature's
cliffs and "pervade its thickets" (94–95). By pursuing Clithero,
Edgar seeks to uncover Clithero's "traces" even while outdistanc-
ing them; he seeks to justify his wilderness incursions by journeying into places his precursor has never been.

Every time Edgar feels daunted by his own limitations, Clithero
teaches him to overcome them. The further Edgar pursues Clithero,
the more he realizes they are not hurrying to a common destination so much as racing one another into the unknown, leading
one another beyond every limit either of them can possibly imagine. Edgar does not want to capture Clithero and return him to
justice; instead, he wants to surpass him, both in his journeying
and his savagery:

> I disdained to be outstripped in this career. All dangers were
> overlooked, and all difficulties defied. I plunged into obscuri-
> ties, and clambered over obstacles, from which, in a different
> state of mind, and with a different object of pursuit, I should
> have recoiled with invincible timidity. When the scene had
> passed, I could not review the perils I had undergone without
> shuddering. (23)

Edgar only experiences the perils of his journey after he has pre-
vailed over them; he transgresses the borderland without really
experiencing his achievement except in retrospect; he reaches into
unknown spaces to find Clithero always-already there. Wherever
Edgar journeys, he discovers in the world's darkest regions a white
man already planting footsteps and legal precedents.

Just as Caleb's penetration of government reveals his own secret
affinity with humanity, Edgar's penetration of the wilderness reveals his affinity with his own imperial nature. In his youth,
Edgar was a compulsive explorer, constantly dreaming about
places in the wilderness which "could never be reached without
wings" (97). As an adult, however, Edgar learns from his pursuit of Clithero that none of humanity's imperial fantasies are
unrealizable:

> Every new excursion indeed added somewhat to my knowl-
> edge. New tracks were pursued, new prospects detected, and
> new summits were gained. My rambles were productive of in-

cessant novelty, though they always terminated in the pros-
pect of limits that could not be overleaped. But none of these
had led me wider from my customary paths than that which
had taken place when in pursuit of Clithero. I had a faint remembrance of the valley, into which I had descended after
him, but till then I had viewed it at a distance, and supposed
it impossible to reach the bottom but by leaping from a precipice some hundred feet in height. The opposite steep seemed
no less inaccessible, and the cavern at the bottom was impervious to any views which my former positions had enabled me
to take of it. (97)

Every time Edgar encounters a boundary he considers "impossible" or "impervious," he proves himself wrong; every limit Edgar encounters marks the boundary of the next space to be "overleaped." Even when he enters Clithero's secret cave he suspects
he has discovered something more awesome than space. He feels
a "sanctity and awe" which he attributes to his own "absolute
and utter loneliness" and finally decides:

It was probable that human feet had never before gained this
recess, that human eyes had never been fixed upon these gush-
ing waters. The aboriginal inhabitants had no motives to lead
them into caves like this, and ponder on the verge of such a
precipice. Their successors were still less likely to have wan-
dered hither. Since the birth of this continent, I was probably
the first who had deviated thus remotely from the customary
paths of men. (103)

Unlike America's "aboriginal inhabitants," Anglo-European explorers possess sufficient "motives" to reach beyond the unreachable; their legs are strong enough to carry them to the "verge" of
the "precipice" and their minds extensive enough to "ponder" the
widest horizons. The gaze of the colonist civilizes the wilderness
the same way it civilizes governments and citizens—by revealing
their deepest truths and buried natures.

By constantly transgressing the "inaccessible" Edgar surrenders
himself to irresistible progress. Every limit he confronts compels
him to transgress it, and every act of transgression leads him to
the brink of another, still further limit to be transgressed. The
only thing Edgar learns from his "utter loneliness" is his own
inherent drive to colonize and appropriate space; his journey

across landscape reveals nothing more than the limitless spaces of Clithero's completely unfathomable personality. While Caleb discovers in Falkland's buried nature a final ground of political equality, Edgar discovers in Clithero a relentless process of imperial expansion.

The existence of the double both reflects and annihilates the integrity of the self.[17] For Godwin, the "double" nature of human beings reminds him that even when individuals are distinguished by economic conditions, their individuality is ultimately subsumed by common reason. In other words, individuals recognize themselves reflected in the eyes of everybody else. The "double" is as much a political as a psychological trope. In Brown's narrative, Edgar sees in Clithero his own lifelong wanderlust, as well as his own innately savage nature. Edgar begins pursuing Clithero because he wants to solve Waldegrave's murder, but he continues pursuing him because they are both driven by the same irresistible nature.

Edgar journeys into the deepest parts of the wilderness to uncover the limits he has yet to transgress and the savage he has always been. Just as Caleb ultimately meets Falkland at the heart of absolute truth, Edgar finally meets Clithero at the heart of the savage wilderness. As Edgar describes him:

> His scanty and coarse garb, had been nearly rent away by brambles and thorns, his arms, bosom and cheek were overgrown and half-concealed by hair. There was somewhat in his attitude and looks denoting more than anarchy of thoughts and passions. His rueful, ghastly, and immoveable eyes, testified not only that his mind was ravaged by despair, but that he was pinched with famine. (104)

Like Caleb in Falkland's courtroom, Edgar discovers a "passion" in Clithero that expresses "more than anarchy"; in one abrupt exclamation, he discovers collective "Man!" in the guise of individual "Clithero!" (105). Clithero describes the border that must be crossed and the collective place men get to on the other side. Men like Edgar reach into the wilderness to recover what they already are.[18]

Men should be admired for their desire to overreach themselves, Edgar decides, and not by whether their overreaching produces good results or not. By seeking to understand Clithero, Edgar begins to understand the faultiness of his own understanding.

Because the final ground of truth can never be firmly established,
Edgar decides that the act of reaching out for truth, however imperfect or misguided, is its own reward. As Clithero warns Edgar
during the first of his spurious confessions, "You, like others, are
blind to the most momentous consequences of your own actions"
(36). And later, still believing Clithero responsible for the death
of Waldegrave, Edgar, like Caleb, empathizes with the criminal
he originally wanted to bring to justice. Since Clithero "acted in
obedience to an impulse which he could not controul," Edgar
wonders whether men like himself can "impute guilt where there
is no design?" (91). If the final map of America has not been established, can one blame men for losing their way? If one can't
blame them, Edgar decides, then one might as well join them.
Edgar concludes that Clithero's intentions must be judged rather
than his actions, because his "crime originated in those limitations which nature has imposed upon human faculties" (92). Individuals are good in proportion to how far they seek to surpass
their limitations, not by how many good deeds they accomplish,
nor by how many good places they discover along the way.

Brown never disavows his Godwinian belief in human perfectibility; like Godwin, he believes that people are capable of perpetually improving themselves and wielding their own subjective
authority in the world—in other words, people don't need anyone
to tell them what truth is. In fact, Brown's notion of truth is so
deeply private, so radically democratic, it never firmly or fully
establishes itself anywhere or in any one person. All people stand
equal in their judgment of the truth, because no permanent, instantly accessible field of knowledge exists to which they can submit. Individuals can only seek truth; they can never finally attain
or utterly know it. The final limit to the westward journey, like
the figure of the American aristocrat, must be constantly deferred. As Mark R. Patterson has explained, readers mistakenly
tend to look for a "singleness of purpose" in Brown or the "*authority* of the author." But this is a sense of authority Brown
never feels obliged to grant us, since truth for him, as for Emerson, is always in a process of *becoming*.[19] Individuals must learn
the truth constantly, just as they must constantly expand the
American map. Brown's texts never reveal any ultimate authority, Patterson concludes, but only "multiplicity of purpose, dis-
continuity, and opacity." They do not establish authority; they
perpetually dispossess it.[20]

American colonial ideology is driven by a sense of perpetual absence; colonists are always driven to find what isn't there and to complete what can never be finished. America never exists as a finished nation but only as an incompletable process of becoming. Sleepwalking pioneers like Edgar and Clithero never uncover America's final border so much as increasing lapses, vacuums, hunger, an infinite series of places where America can never be found. From Clara Wieland to Arthur Mervyn, Brown's protagonists seek to penetrate obscurities, only to become lost in still deeper ones. Every time Arthur thinks he finally comprehends Welbeck's character and intentions, Welbeck (like Clithero) vanishes to become somebody else entirely. Clara Wieland penetrates secret rooms and histories only to discover Carwin the biloquist's fantastic and diverting projections. Nobody ever learns the truth about anyone or anything in a Brown novel until everybody (including the reader) has forgotten what they were looking for in the first place.

Clithero's position has been drained of meaning in order to institute a constant process of meaning-production. While Falkland's padlocked trunk ultimately discloses the conspiracy of government, Clithero's trunk (like Brown's narrative) is "divided into numerous compartments" but betrays nothing "of moment" (117). Disappointed by the trunk in Clithero's room, Edgar hurries back to the elm, where he digs up another of Clithero's boxes. This one at least contains *something*—Mrs. Lorimer's written "performance" of "her genius and her virtue," a diary that records her undying devotion to her dissolute brother, Wiatte; however, even this personal confession does nothing to aid Edgar's progress either in solving the mystery of Waldegrave's murder or the mystery of Clithero's character. Putting down Mrs. Lorimer's confession, Edgar abruptly chases off again after the always-disappearing Clithero, but the Irishman has already vanished, thus leading Edgar to the brink of "dark and untried paths" that even Edgar hasn't explored before.

The succession of absences progresses at an alarming rate: Edgar discovers that Waldegrave's somewhat heretical philosophical papers have vanished from the place Edgar himself has hidden them. Documents, boxes, psychologies, philosophies, mysteries: the more Edgar investigates, the less he discloses, and the less he discloses, the further he pursues his investigation into the dense

wilderness. Absence engages absence, and the power that generates this weird progress into darkness is itself geographical, one
which Edgar claims can casually "waft" even his own most
closely guarded secrets "over the ocean or the mountains," enlist-
ing Edgar in "a fruitless and eternal search" for them (135). Edgar
discovers this power deep in his own heart, compelling him to
hide Waldegrave's papers from all eyes—including his own—during one of his own bouts of sleepwalking. In the same way he has
imagined conspiracies at work both in Clithero's mind and in the
wilderness, Edgar creates the very absences he tirelessly seeks to
explore. The purpose of pursuit is not to divulge truth but to explore territory.

Faced with these final darknesses—empty boxes, unreachable
caverns, even the "secret motives" of his best friend, Waldegrave—Edgar journeys into the deepest regions of mind and
space. As in *Caleb Williams*, the horizontal and vertical narratives of *Edgar Huntly* intersect in a prison, a place of radically
subjective geography. Carried off further than ever before by his
own somnambulating body, Edgar awakes in a chamber pervaded
by "the murkiest and most impenetrable gloom"; it is the very
heart of absence, a place which prohibits "every particle of light"
and replaces it with "palpable obscurity" (160–161). Here he is
stalked by a panther whose wide, undeviating gaze recalls Falkland's "lynx-eyed jealousy," and Edgar cannot help but imagine
himself "the victim of some tyrant who had thrust me into a dun-
geon of his fortress, and left me no power to determine whether
he intended I should perish with famine, or linger out a long life
in hopeless imprisonment" (161–162).

Where Caleb penetrates the heart of aristocracy to discover the
walls of a prison, Edgar awakes in a prison to discover the traces
of an aristocracy that has already vanished. Wherever Edgar arrives the truth has already been and gone. Just as he refuses to let
Clithero outdistance him, he "disdain[s] to be out-done in perspi-
cacity by the lynx, in his sure-footed instinct by the roe, or in
patience under hardship, and contention with fatigue, by the Mo-
hawk" (212). By overreaching Clithero, Edgar wants to prove he
is more savage than savages; for him, succeeding and *exceeding*
mean precisely the same thing. Edgar has "ever aspired to transcend the rest of animals in all that is common to the rational
and brute, as well as in all by which they are distinguished from

each other" (212). By transgressing space and identity, Edgar ultimately glimpses a "passage into new forms, overleaping the bars of time and space" (239).[21]

Edgar Huntly is about the endless process of recovering human nature and exploiting America's abundance, not about solving crimes. Ultimately Brown solves Waldegrave's murder almost as an afterthought and hastily clarifies Clithero's history in time for Clithero to mysteriously vanish again. Waldegrave's murder, along with a series of colonial misfortunes, is traced back to an elderly woman known as Deb whose property Edgar casually trespassed on his way back from the wilderness. Deb has been battling the colonists for years, refusing to let them take her land, which she claims belongs to her by ancestral right. Edgar decides to call her "Queen Mab" because of her "pretensions to royalty, the wildness of her aspect and garb, her shrivelled and diminutive form, a constitution that seemed to defy the ravages of time and the influence of the elements; her age, which some did not scruple to affirm exceeded a hundred years, her romantic solitude and mountainous haunts" (209). Queen Mab's property represents the final scene of Edgar's colonial transgressions. He trespasses her "estate" with the submerged awareness of a sleepwalker dreaming into existence his own savage life. By her "pretensions to royalty," Queen Mab represents both a final destination and a perilous afterthought. By becoming like an Indian, Edgar stumbles onto the ultimate ground of his relentless colonial enterprise; he exceeds the Indians by exceeding himself and collapses unconscious outside Deb's hut, awakening later to be mistaken by Sarsefield's posse as just another rampaging Indian. Like Caleb, Edgar identifies with the object of his own pursuit; he ends up committing the same savage crimes he originally sought to punish. Edgar dreams of taking property from "savages" by being a better savage than they are; he trespasses Indian property in order to become an Indian himself. At the conclusion of *Edgar Huntly*, Brown still hasn't learned how to bring the narrative of transgression to a stable resolution, primarily because he hasn't looked at America as a historical enterprise yet, a place of fixed spaces and permanent laws. The American novel is still awaiting Cooper, who will teach it the meaning of property.

3

James Fenimore Cooper and the Return of the King

Representing History in The Pioneers

The inefficiency of the effort to subvert things by names, is shown in the fact that, in all civilized communities, there is a class of men, who silently and quietly recognize each other, as gentlemen; who associate together freely and without reserve, and who admit each other's claims without scruple or distrust. This class may be limited by prejudice and arbitrary enactments, as in Europe, or it may have no other rules than those of taste, sentiment and the silent laws of usage, as in America.

—James Fenimore Cooper,
The American Democrat[1]

The power of transgressing nature is itself within nature.

—Jacques Derrida, Of Grammatology[2]

As Cooper himself quickly points out, *The Pioneers* does not present so much as re-present the colonization of Otsego in upper New York. Although Cooper bases the novel on his own family history, he transforms that history into a symbolic narrative that transcends historical events. By lending to the raw events of history a rigid formal coherence or "story," Cooper establishes an invisible government over them. By imposing form on the past, Cooper can decide what history is and which parts of it are worth remembering.

In his 1832 introduction to *The Pioneers*, Cooper explains that in this, his third novel, he provides more "general picture" than "literal fact":

> The author is very sensible, that had he confined himself to the latter, always the most effective, as it is the most valuable mode of conveying knowledge of this nature, he would have made a far better book. But, in commencing to describe scenes, and perhaps he may add characters, that were so familiar to his own youth, there was a constant temptation to delineate that which he had known rather than that which he might have imagined. This rigid adhesion to truth, an indispensable requisite in history and travels, destroys the charm of fiction, for all that is necessary to be conveyed to the mind by the latter had better be done by delineations of principles and of characters in their classes, than by a too fastidious attention to originals.[3]

For Cooper, the "charm of fiction" lies in its ability to depict abstract "principles" and "classes" rather than simply recount "fastidious" details. The properly "imagined" novel represents real events and information by imposing (or revealing) their inherent formal clarity; the novelist represents individual men and women by revealing their "principles" of action and their "classes" of human character. The job of the novelist is not to describe daily life but to remind readers of the world's general forms and orderly landscapes.[4] Cooper does not believe, like Jefferson or Paine, that all men are created equal; instead, he repeatedly implies that an individual's existence is determined by his or her occupation (in fact, he often spends pages describing a character's job or social background long before he even mentions his or her name). For Cooper, individuals are conditioned by their class in the same way governments are conditioned by human principles.

In Cooper's *The Pioneers*, colonists don't civilize the wilderness so much as the wilderness proves itself implicitly civilized long before Europeans ever get there. The reader's gaze is never permitted to observe the landscape freshly as an original settler, for his or her view is always already, even before it is experienced, acculturated and formalized. During the opening pages of *The Pioneers*, the reader travels through "a succession of hills and dales" to discover that civilization got here first (15). The wild scene already "possesses" a "picturesque character," an inherent capacity to be artistically framed.[5] As the passage develops, the reader uncovers a rigidly formalized, already-civilized, and quintessentially static Cooperian "landscape":

> The vales are narrow, rich, and cultivated; with a stream uniformly winding through each. Beautiful and thriving villages are found interspersed along the margins of the small lakes, or situated at those points of the streams which are favourable to manufacturing; and neat and comfortable farms, with every indication of wealth about them, are scattered profusely through the vales, and even to the mountain tops. Roads diverge in every direction, from the even and graceful bottoms of the valleys, to the most rugged and intricate passes of the hills. Academies, and minor edifices of learning, meet the eye of the stranger, at every few miles, as he winds his way through this uneven territory; and places for the worship of God, abound with that frequency which characterizes a moral and reflecting people, and with that variety of exterior and canonical government which flows from unfettered liberty of conscience. (15)

Cooper's "stranger" discovers in the wilderness schools, churches, and farms a landscape which has already been made "cultivated," "uniform," and "graceful." It is a landscape formalized by the "moral" schemes of a "reflecting people," one which exteriorizes innate human properties. Like landscape paintings or pages in books, even the lakes possess "margins" that are "favourable to manufacturing." Otsego's "uneven territory" contains roads and irrigated fields, while civilization itself is described as a sort of supplement, an "exterior" system of government.

Revolution presupposes the American Constitution, Cooper's description suggests, just as some original moment of colonial trespass presupposes the successful settlement. Cooper's description of Templeton eventually suggests that the town has not simply established physical dominion over nature but Republican principles over people. As Cooper continues:

> In short, the whole district is hourly exhibiting how much can be done, in even a rugged country, and with a severe climate, under the dominion of mild laws, and where every man feels a direct interest in the prosperity of a commonwealth, of which he knows himself to form a part. The expedients of the pioneers who first broke ground in the settlement of this country, are succeeded by the permanent improvements of the yeoman, who intends to leave his remains to moulder under the sod which he tills, or, perhaps, of the son, who, born in the land, piously wishes to linger around the grave of his father. (15–16)[6]

The American "commonwealth," Cooper suggests, was founded by and upon a series of transgressions committed by the now deceased "father." These transgressions of the fathers, what Cooper often refers to as the lawless "expedients" of the pioneers, become totemized as property—that grave-side where succeeding generations establish a permanent home and history. The subversion of aristocracy and the invasion of the American wilderness are events which make each other happen. It is the successful revolution against Britain, sanctioned by the "peace of 1783," that allows Americans to develop "their widely extended dominions," just as it is the revolution's "unfettered liberty" that causes a "magical change in the power and condition" of American commerce (16).

American colonists and revolutionaries always bury their originating moment of violence underneath monuments to their fathers.[7] Bourgeois revolution, in other words, establishes authority by sanctifying transgression as an act that occurs in either the past or the wilderness. As he grows older, Cooper never really abandons his revolutionary enthusiasms, as some critics have argued; in fact, even in works as early as *The Pioneers* he defends the American Revolution by claiming that since it has been achieved once, it never has to happen again—especially not by anybody who wants what Cooper's family already owns.[8] As Cooper wrote in his last work, an unfinished history of New York, "men accomplish more in the earliest stages of society when perfectly unfettered, than when brought under the control of those

principles and regulations which alone can render society permanently secure or happy."⁹ Once the "unfettered" accomplish-
ments and "expedients" of pioneers and revolutionaries have se-
cured new governments and properties, succeeding generations
can settle down to being "secure" and "happy," allowing themselves to be "brought under the control" of "principles and regulations." Revolution creates a new nation which does not require
any further revolutions; by breaking laws and freeing people,
America creates a nation strong enough to place freedom under
restraint.

Midway through *The Pioneers*, Judge Temple informs his daughter Elizabeth that she, like most members of her generation, cannot recognize the history that surrounds her. As Judge Temple
explains, when Elizabeth encounters "the loads of produce that
issue out of every wild path in these mountains," she doesn't realize that only five years previously "the tenants of these woods
were compelled to eat the scanty fruits of the forest" (233). By
enduring scarcity and hardships, the original pioneers enjoyed
an Edenic communion with nature; but since then, a pioneer
culture of self-sufficiency has been transformed into a civilized
economy of excess.

Judge Temple goes on to recall that he was not the first white
man to discover Otsego so much as the first to invest it with
imaginative form and potential. He dubs the site where he first
glimpsed his new property Mount Vision because "the sight that
there met my eyes seemed to me as the deceptions of a dream"
(235). Judge Temple dreams of more than a pioneer colony; he
dreams of discovering in nature his own Colonial Father. Like
Edgar Huntly, Temple transgresses nature to find one of his ancestors already there.¹⁰

Judge Temple recalls that on his first visit to Mount Vision

"I had met many deer, gliding through the woods, in my journey; but not the vestige of a man could I trace, during my
progress, nor from my elevated observatory. No clearing, no
hut, none of the winding roads that are now to be seen, were
there; nothing but mountains rising behind mountains, and
the valley, with its surface of branches, enlivened here and
there with the faded foliage of some tree, that parted from its
leaves with more than ordinary reluctance. Even the Susquehanna was then hid, by the height and density of the forest."

"And were you alone?" asked Elizabeth;—"passed you the night in that solitary state?"

"Not so, my child," returned her father. (235–236)

Like the Susquehanna, the source of everything natural, human faces are obscured (but never erased) by the forest's density. Pioneers invade the wilderness to reveal their own symbolic reflection, which, like the disheveled figure of Brown's Clithero, represents both the individual and the idea. The moment Elizabeth mistakenly supposes her father to be the lone hero of his tale, Judge Temple recalls the figure of Natty, who stands behind the wilderness like a deed or a legal precedent, representing the wilderness's entire history of native precursors. At first sight, Natty's hut resembles "a habitation of the Indians" (236). But Natty provides Temple food to eat and a place to sleep, and on the property he already possesses Temple discovers a tenant already residing. The tenant will not only make Judge Temple feel at home but eventually help him establish his legal proprietorship beyond any reasonable doubt.

Judge Temple tames the wilderness with "mild laws" (laws themselves adapted from British monarchical statutes, as Brook Thomas has observed) only after subverting the local aristocracy of name and helping to replace it with an aristocracy of merit.[11] Early in the novel, Cooper explains that, upon relocating in America, Marmaduke's family learned they could "depend rather on their hereditary possessions than on their own powers" (31). By depending on inheritance for their status and privileges, the Temples grew smug and indolent, "and in the third generation, they had descended to a point, below which, it is barely possible for honesty, intellect, and sobriety, to fall" (31). Eventually, however, the Temples learned to establish themselves in the New World by realizing that

> the same pride of family, that had, by its self-satisfied indolence, conduced to aid their fall, now became a principle to stimulate them to endeavor to rise again. The feeling, from being morbid, was changed to a healthful and active desire to emulate the character, the condition, and, peradventure, the wealth, of their ancestors also. It was the father of our new acquaintance, the Judge, who first began to re-ascend in the scale of society; and in this undertaking he was not a little assisted by a marriage, which aided in furnishing the means

of educating his only son, in a rather better manner than the
low state of the common schools of Pennsylvania could promise, or than had been the practice in the family, for the two or
three preceding generations. (31)

To a large extent, noble families fail only when their inner
characters are weak. Judge Temple's family history marks the postrevolutionary shift in the definition of exemplary families described by Jay Fliegelman as a movement from patriarchy to pa-
ternalism, from a system in which fathers rule by virtue of being
fathers, to one in which rulers justify their authority by being
good, benevolent, and fatherlike.[12] Rather than rely on the ac-
complishments of their ancestors, the Temples begin to rise again
through their own "endeavor." They work hard, marry well, and
properly educate their children.

American politicians, from John Quincy Adams to Thomas Jefferson, considered revolution a means of replacing "hereditary"
families with a new type of aristocrat who was both more "natural" than his or her predecessors and more financially productive.
The "nature" of individuals, in effect, was supposed to subvert
the inherited "name" of families, allowing the signified to claim
its rightful dominance over the signifier in a sort of linguistic revolt, establishing a "truer" order of signification in which the fullness of nature determines the meaning of words and words do not
repress or limit the meaning of nature. This subversion of "name"
by "essence" does not necessarily deprivilege specific families so
much as redefine the conditions of privilege. As John Quincy Adams proclaims shortly after the American Revolution: "a nobility
must and will exist though without the name, as really as in
countries where it is hereditary; for the people, by their elections,
will continue the government generally in the same families from
generation to generation."[13] Individual families prove their aristocratic character through hard work and good deeds, they then
pass on the qualities (and not simply the name) of aristocracy to
their children. It's what they earn and accomplish that matters,
not the historic associations stirred up by their thin names and
titles. Judge Temple must prove his personal value every day
through good works and sound judgments, relying on his "own
powers" and disdaining the "self-satisfied indolence" of his dead
ancestors. Though he acquires most of his property by confiscating Tory estates, Judge Temple makes it profitable through his
own hard work and ambition, ultimately developing his personal

"vision" of a frontier community from a mountaintop overlooking the same dispossessed natives who will do their best to make him feel at home.

Although Cooper describes the conflict between Temple and Effingham as a conflict between Loyalist and Republican (an advocacy of "crown" as opposed to an advocacy of "people"), their friendship supersedes the temperamental vicissitudes of class and fortune. Their political differences are never more than "a subject of amicable dispute between them," and right up until the battle of Lexington they share an implicit faith in one another so genuine that even when the political world makes them enemies, Mr. Effingham still entrusts "to Marmaduke for safe keeping, all his valuable effects and papers" (36). Only the outbreak of war affects their relationship, causing a break of "all intercourse" between them and a "cautious reserve" on the part of Marmaduke. For Marmaduke and Effingham, revolution doesn't initiate violent conflict but only a break in correspondence during which all of Temple's letters to Oliver's father are "returned unopened" (440). But even during this long silence, Marmaduke continues to honor his pledge to the reactionary Effingham, multiplying the value of his properties "in a ten-fold ratio" by means of his own "strong and practiced reason" (37).

Judge Temple's revolutionary success is made possible both by Effingham's disappearance and the emergence of new laws, laws which redistribute monarchically granted properties among revolutionary citizens—a procedure originally proposed by Tom Paine as a way of settling Britain's trade debts to the colonies. While Temple remains loyal both to his country and his vanished reactionary partner, he also keeps a constant eye out for "his own interests; for, when the estates of the adherents of the crown fell under the hammer, by the acts of confiscation, he appeared in New York, and became the purchaser of extensive possessions, at, comparatively, low prices" (36). Judge Temple's confiscation of these properties begins to seem legitimate and natural to other settlers, Cooper explains, because of the "frequency of the transgressions in others" (36); and although at first Judge Temple's neighbors ridicule him because he "wrested by violence" his lands from their original owner, his character is subsequently vindicated by sound financial management and his deep sense of personal responsibility to the vanished Effinghams. Such legal transgressions help settle the wilderness and make it

both more productive for America and less productive for Britain. But once the initial transgression has been committed, it
must help imagine a world more stable and secure than the
one which allowed it to occur. It must imagine a world, in fact,
where its originating moment of violence cannot be completely
remembered.

After the revolution, Judge Temple's dedication to innate "principles" and "practical reason" helps him increase the value of
his lands until he is "among the most wealthy and important of
his countrymen" (37). Because Cooper's "natural" aristocrats believe that individual character denotes the true meaning of property, Temple disdains the "speculator" who arbitrarily transforms
property values to turn a quick profit; because it is always "fluctuating and uncertain," the speculator's haphazard "pursuit of
commerce" does not develop properties but only changes their
value, creating a world of unstable signification. Cooper is more
Jeffersonian than capitalist, believing that revolution's transgression of property rights will establish a more permanent system of
political and economic order; the reified *process* of transgression
valorized by a free-market economy makes him deeply uneasy.
Cooper only wants one revolution, and it has to have happened
yesterday.

Aristocracy as Estate

*English law—as authority, as legitimizing precedent, as
embodied principle, and as the framework of historical
understanding—stood side by side with Enlightenment
rationalism in the minds of the Revolutionary generation.*

  —Bernard Bailyn, *The Ideological
    Origins of the American Revolution*[14]

*We live in a world of transgressions and selfishness, and no
pictures that represent us otherwise can be true, though,
happily for human nature, gleanings of that pure spirit in
whose likeness man has been fashioned are to be seen,
relieving its deformities and mitigating if not excusing its
crimes.*

  —James Fenimore Cooper, *The Deerslayer*[15]

Cooper's novels never depict historical progress so much as a synchronous mosaic of past and present, aristocrat and bourgeois, Indian and colonist. In Cooper's landscape, the Indian's world doesn't prefigure the conflict between British crown and colonial republic but reflects it, thus naturalizing revolution as a force endemic to all cultures—like truth, say, or justice. In *The Pioneers*, Cooper's discussion of Templeton's financial development leads into a summary history of the "two great nations of Indians." Cooper explains that the political disputes between these tribes were always "marked," much like the disputes between aristocrat and bourgeois,

> by a difference in language, as well as by repeated and bloody wars, [and] they never were known to amalgamate, until after the power and inroads of the whites had reduced some of the tribes to a state of dependence, that rendered not only their political, but, considering the wants and habits of a savage, their animal existence also, extremely precarious.
>
> These two great divisions consisted, on the one side, of the Five, or, as they were afterwards called, the Six Nations, and their allies; and, on the other, of the Lenni Lenape, or Delawares. (83)

For Cooper, humanity's natural state manifests a class dualism, one dividing mongrel mob from Old Family. According to Cooper, the Delawares suffer linguistic aggressions from the Six Nations, who repeatedly refer to them as "women." Eventually, this oppression of false words leads to tribal conflict about the same time American colonies begin revolting against Britain. Cooper continues:

> This state of things continued until the war of the revolution, when the Lenni Lenape formally asserted their independence, and fearlessly declared, that they were again men. But, in a government, so peculiarly republican as the Indian polity, it was not, at all times, an easy task, to restrain its members within the rules of the nation. Several fierce and renowned warriors, of the Mohegans, finding the conflict with the whites to be in vain, sought a refuge with their Grandfather, and brought with them the feelings and principles, that had so long distinguished them in their own tribe. These chieftains kept alive, in some measure, the martial spirit of the Dela-

wares; and would, at times, lead small parties against their ancient enemies, or such other foes as incurred their resentment. (84)

In his retelling of Indian conflict (one he reiterates many times throughout the Leatherstocking Saga), Cooper describes an inverted image of the American Revolution. Just as the Mohicans "formally" assert their "independence" by redefining the terms of their own "manhood"—their avowal, in a sense, of innate "feelings" and "principles" as inalienable as those of the Constitution—they revolt not only against other Indian tribes but against white colonialism as well. Defined as a racially homogeneous "nation" opposed by a fragmentary collection of independent states, the Mohicans/Delawares don't simply represent either the British aristocracy or the revolutionary bourgeoisie so much as the ideological conflation of both: they describe, in fact, a native version of Cooper's "natural" aristocrat. Like either a tyrannical ruler or an unruly mob of democrats, the Six Nations attempt to impose false authority over an ancient race. The Delawares revolt against the Six Nations in order to recover the genetic authority of their own ancestors—both their literal father, who is an Indian chief, and their symbolic grandfather, who is a British monarch.

The Delaware political hierarchy is defined in familial terms, naturalizing Europe's patriarchal monarchy and politicizing America's native wisdom. Like the "natural aristocrats" of Templeton (Natty, Oliver, Chingachgook) who must endure the democratic rabble's "wasty ways," the Delawares are oppressed by an impure conglomeration of mixed races and discordant languages. Where the bourgeoisie subvert monarchical institutions and reestablish their own more natural democratic principles, the Delawares subvert the lying Mingoes to reestablish the original unity of their tribe. To make this clearer in a rather reductive diagram:

NATURAL ARISTOCRACY	ORIGINAL UNITY OF TRIBES
Aristocracy	Six Nations/European colonists
Bourgeoisie	Delawares

The Delawares transgress bad government in order to recall who they were before bad government came along; and colonial revolutionaries transgress British rule in order to recall their own native authority. The Lenni Lenape try to prevent the Mohicans

from achieving a unified government, just as the European aristocracy tries to prevent the bourgeoisie from establishing natural
consensus.

As the first of Cooper's "last" Mohicans, Chingachgook, "the
sole representative of this once renowned family," represents the
fall of the true Indian aristocracy at the same time the rapproche-
ment between Judge Temple and Oliver Effingham reunifies colonial America's class antagonists. Monarchical qualities are as-
cribed to the Chingachgook-Temple-Effingham group in order to
create a symbolic accord between the three major American rep-
resentatives of tenure and privilege; as a result, Cooper hopes to
control America's revolutionary excesses with what Donald Pease
has labeled a "visionary compact"—a symbolic resolution of
political conflict.[16] The Constitution was designed to formalize,
and thus symbolically control, entrepreneurial and imperialist
excesses; without it, Americans feared their confederation would
degenerate into an unending series of revolts and piratical land
grabs, such as those which regularly turned eighteenth-century
state borders into battlegrounds.[17]

In postrevolutionary Templeton, petty officials such as Richard
Jones and Hiram Doolittle orbit Judge Temple's house as if they
"were the nobles of Templeton, as Marmaduke was its king" (42).
Yet Temple's civil authority, like Falkland's, poses a mystery to
be solved; once Temple's appearances have been penetrated, his
true status may be better described by Richard's reference to him
as a "duke," since Temple, like Richard and Hiram, himself acts as
a sort of sublunary official to the displaced Effinghams. In the
Effinghams, Cooper creates his vision of ideal authority, one
which both precedes and succeeds the revolution, framing it like
a sort of landscape or a declaration of principles. It is a family in
which the senile and disintegrated aristocratic grandfather is su-
perseded by the youthful, intrepid Oliver, who acts as both an
inheritor of family title and a frontiersman of supreme natural
abilities. Though Major Effingham's return signals the rebirth of
the Effingham empire, it is his grandson Oliver who proves to be,
as Elizabeth correctly observes, "in secret a king" (279).

In order to solve the mystery of Templeton's secret government,
Cooper's narrative, like Brown's, journeys away from civilization
and into the wilderness, returning Judge Temple to the scene of
Natty's hut, where the symbolic interpenetration of aristocrat and

commoner becomes totemized as property. While Natty's hut appears at first rustic and isolated, it actually contains three hidden, metaphorically unified bodies of displaced authority: the pioneer, the Indian, and the king. As an effective force in Cooper's work, the king must be eliminated. As a dream, however, the king must be preserved.[18]

As Natty warns Elizabeth late in the novel, he plans to revenge himself against the "righteous judge" by revealing the forest's secrets: "The moment of concealment is over, Miss Temple. By this time to-morrow, I shall remove a veil that perhaps it has been weakness to keep around me and my affairs so long" (424). Revealing secrets, Natty avows, will not only undermine Judge Temple's authority as sole legitimate proprietor of Templeton but will increase Natty's own depleted physical strength, lending him the momentum he requires to continue westward, colonize new territories, and escape civilization's legal restraints. Judge Temple fails as king because he succeeds as moral authority, fulfilling his responsibilities both to the community he governs and the displaced Tory landlords he gratefully welcomes home. Natty, on the other hand, the purest of democrats, makes both property and knowledge public but never accepts any political responsibility for them. Represented by Natty, the most radical form of democracy is more motion than place, more story than character; it never stops moving and never rests anywhere long enough to establish its own permanent version of government. Cooper's ideal pioneers disappear into the West and the past simultaneously; meanwhile, the democracy they leave behind must reconcile itself with aristocracy in order to achieve equilibrium and permanence and thus forget or defer the disorienting violence which first struck it into existence.

At the beginning, middle, and end of *The Pioneers*, Natty justifies his killing of a deer by appealing to the unwritten (and unwriteable) doctrine of "natural" rights.[19] But while claiming he has the right to kill wild game according to personal needs, Natty's frequent appeals to natural law only serve to distract public attention from his true license. Since Natty secretly serves as gentleman-at-arms to Major Effingham, he functions not only as servant to the servant of the king but as aide-de-camp to Templeton's true owner and lawgiver. Without this figure of Major Effingham preserved behind the screen of nature, Natty's role as "noble savage" threatens to degenerate into a chaotic rush of more random and self-interested "expedients"; if individuals can act freely at all times, then society will suffer mad citizens firing guns at random pigeons in the sky or dragging home weirfuls of fish they can't eat. As Oliver says, just before Natty's hut is violated by Judge Temple's deputies, "We have all been equally transgressors of the law" (299–300). In order to create community, citizens must establish a symbolic sense of order which will embrace former transgressions and prevent them from happening again. Natty does not belong to this community of symbolic order; he belongs to the moment that occurs just before such a community is reestablished.

By penetrating the false veil of Judge Temple's authority, Natty reveals Oliver's grandfather, Major Effingham, who secretly possesses legitimate rule not only over civilized Templeton and uncivilized Mohicans but over the subversive, half-civilized figures of Natty and Oliver as well. Major Effingham, who appears just in time to save Templeton's citizens from their increasingly rampant democracy, represents a symbolic hybrid of savage and gentleman. His "dress," Cooper explains, "was composed of such fabrics as none but the wealthiest classes wear, but was threadbare and patched; and on his feet were placed a pair of moccasins, ornamented in the best manner of Indian ingenuity" (436). Major Effingham represents both the return of the king and the return of the disenfranchised Indian. The natural king, along with the Indian, has returned in order to validate the very act of violence which dispossessed him; he is the king who legitimates his own subversion, the Indian who not only forgives the robbers of his home but provides them a key to its back door.

Both Judge Temple and his sheriff are rendered "mute" by Natty's revelation of the major (437). Their silence admits a new government in which language fails to operate. Though their words once established law and ownership, their voicelessness now describes the absence of their authority and the reemergence of a sublime, indisputable monarch of symbolic property. In response to Temple's laws and the mob's rude pretensions, Major Effingham's archetypal figure reappears from the world of nature to make laws real again. The scene of the major's reappearance deserves to be quoted at length:

> At length the decrepit stranger, turning his vacant looks from
> face to face, made a feeble attempt to rise, while a faint smile

crossed his wasted face, like an habitual effort at courtesy, as he said, in a hollow, tremulous voice—

"Be pleased to be seated, gentlemen. The council will open immediately. Each one who loves a good and virtuous king, will wish to see these colonies continue loyal. Be seated—I pray you, be seated, gentlemen. The troops shall halt for the night."

"This is the wandering of insanity!" said Marmaduke; "who will explain this scene?"

"No, sir," said Edwards, firmly, "'tis only the decay of nature; who is answerable for its pitiful condition, remains to be shown."

"Will the gentlemen dine with us, my son?" said the old stranger, turning to a voice that he both knew and loved. "Order a repast suitable for his Majesty's officers. You know we have the best of game always at command."

"Who is this man?" asked Marmaduke, in a hurried voice, in which the dawnings of conjecture united with interest to put the question.

"This man!" returned Edwards, calmly, his voice, however, gradually rising as he proceeded; "this man, sir, whom you behold hid in caverns, and deprived of every thing that can make life desirable, was once the companion and counsellor of those who ruled your country. This man, whom you see, helpless and feeble, was once a warrior, so brave and fearless, that even the intrepid natives gave him the name of the Fire-Eater. This man, whom you now see destitute of even the ordinary comfort of a cabin in which to shelter his head, was once the owner of great riches; and, Judge Temple, he was the rightful proprietor of this very soil on which we stand. This man was the father of"—

"This, then," cried Marmaduke, with a powerful emotion, "this, then, is the lost Major Effingham!"

"Lost, indeed," said the youth, fixing a piercing eye on the other. (436–437)

Not lost, Oliver's ironic glance indicates, so much as disavowed. Major Effingham dreams of feudal estates where monarchical armies eat their approved meat and colonial citizens remain loyal forever to their king. The major dreams of a past that is always about to happen again, a dream in which king, major, Natty,

Judge Temple, Oliver, and Chingachgook's forlorn ghost pose eternally in a snapshot of frozen time—historical process aestheticized into family portrait. Major Effingham represents the fallen king who has been readmitted to the home where he has always belonged. Through his grandson the major is reborn as a symbolic figure of both royal legitimacy and natural rights; he embraces and effaces the absence of his son and Oliver's father, the actual victim of revolutionary violence. Together with his grandson, the major's renascent figure describes the return of a king who is at once "decrepit" and youthful, insane and rational, "decayed" and regenerate. Just as Edgar Huntly discovers both "Man" and "Clithero" in remote caverns, so Cooper's spelunkers discover both "Man" and "king."

Like the structure of *The Pioneers* or the major's own autumnal reason, the fall and rise of aristocracy describes an eternal, seasonal cycle of decay and regeneration.[20] Judge Temple's silence readmits the return of the king's voice, just as Oliver's "piercing eye" recognizes Temple as both the revolutionary usurper of family estate and his own sublunary official who, like the persistently noisy Richard, has been presumptuously trying to exceed his assigned role. The revolutionary does not depose the king but joins with him in a weird symbiosis. The major wears two styles of dress just as he carries both Indian and European names, and he arrives to solve the problem of government caused by Natty's slaying of the deer. Natty's innocence is not determined by an appeal to natural laws, as most commentators argue, but by the emergence of the major's dreams of a redeemed aristocracy, one in which Natty acts as one of "his Majesty's officers" in order to provide game for the king's "troops." In his symbolic role of the "Fire-Eater," Major Effingham swallows up the threats of democratic agitation and rampant capitalism which have burned down not only the forests around Templeton but the Wall Street warehouse district in *Home as Found*. Democrats, by threatening to mindlessly change identities and property values, manifest a sort of primal lawlessness, a chaos of fire and destruction which can only be nullified by the major's reappearance. The major's presence recalls the past of both primal Indians and exalted king, instituting a permanent system of proprietorship over Templeton which resolves conflicts between bourgeois and aristocrat, Loyalist and Tory, nature and government. He creates a stable landscape and a sense of permanence invulnerable to the flames of radical democracy.

As Thomas Philbrick has argued, the Mohicans' symbolic adoption of Major Effingham legitimates the theft of Indian lands according to British laws of primogeniture.[21] By thus "inheriting" Templeton, Oliver heals the original violence of both revolution and imperialism. The Indians, like Judge Temple, are not usurped; rather, they submit obligingly to fair laws.

Cooper's work wrestles out of revolution and imperialism a stable, enduring world to which a new aristocracy can be safely readmitted. By preserving the king as a symbolic body, Cooper wants to distinguish America from the revolutionary French, whose violent domestic and imperial excesses were creating a great deal of Federalist anxiety in Cooper's time. For Cooper, revolution cannot be promoted without instituting a system of order and meaning which will assure that revolution doesn't happen again. The properties of Indians and aristocrats can only be reassigned if stronger and more incontrovertible property rights are established as a result.

The Pioneers is set during the period of the French Revolution in order to illustrate America's better way of handling things; as opposed to the French, American revolutionary violence establishes order through class reconciliation, without degenerating into a mob of indistinguishably equal men. Early in *The Pioneers* Cooper refers to France's revolution as "that commotion, which afterwards shook her political institutions to the centre" (96). In the same passage referring to France's "commotion," Cooper recalls Major Effingham's "King's letter patent," which, during the revolution, Judge Temple violates by confiscating Effingham's property. Cooper's intention here is clear: to remind Americans that the subversion of aristocratic property could very well lead to the sort of anarchy unleashed in France, especially if that initial act of subversion does not create sound laws and indisputable authority. As Judge Temple himself later explains, "The French, since they have beheaded their king, have done nothing but fight" (160–161). When citizens violate authority, they create a world where violence never stops; since nobody has more power than anybody else, transgressions escalate. By killing their king, the French have become as "bloodthirsty as bull-dogs . . . rushing from one act of licentiousness to another" (160). As the French expatriate Monsieur Le Quoi proclaims, by allowing their revolution to exceed all bounds, the French Jacobins have proven themselves to be mere "monstres"!

America succeeds where Europe fails by directing its revolutionary violence away from itself. By overturning Judge Temple's authority Natty helps institute the Effingham family's greater one, but by proving himself an effective revolutionary force he becomes too dangerous to keep around; as a result, there's nowhere Natty can go except west. Once Oliver regains both legal and natural primogeniture over Templeton, Natty decides his own brand of personal justice is incompatible with community law, so he decides to journey out to the "Big-Lakes," where he expects to find "the best of hunting, and a great range, without a white man on it, unless it may be one like myself" (453). Like *Edgar Huntly*, Natty cannot conceive of the western lands without imagining someone like himself already out there. By violating Templeton's laws and departing westward, Natty glorifies his transgressive nature while directing it safely away from the settlements. Like most of Cooper's characters, Natty does not function as an individual so much as a cultural or mythological type, representing all that is "foremost in that band of Pioneers, who are opening the way for the march of the nation across the continent" (456). Instead of replaying America's original act of colonial violence over and over again, Natty retreats into a dream of history in which transgressive violence is sublimated and made clean again by eternal westward progress.

Like *Edgar Huntly*, the Leatherstocking Saga journeys farther into both the wilderness and humanity's savage past. As several critics have shown, the more anxious Cooper becomes to establish ownership over his father's estate in Cooperstown, the further back he investigates the career of his most popular creation, Natty Bumppo.[22] In Natty's youthful incarnation as Deerslayer, Cooper imagines a legal precedent which predates the rude masses of both actual Cooperstown and fictional Templeton. In effect, Cooper is imaginatively justifying his rights not only to physical land but to the commodification of the "picturesque," and this anxiety about both literal and figurative property becomes especially intense for Cooper during the so-called Three Mile Point controversy, when the Cooperstown population claimed they possessed "natural" rights to picnic on Cooper's

property and enjoy its sublime view. Beauty, the public claimed,
belonged to no single individual but to all humanity. According
to Cooper, however, common men and women don't implicitly
deserve a clear view of nature's beauty but have to earn it and
prove they have earned it over a period of generations. The mob
of rude, disenfranchised masses neither recognize the integrity of
nature nor respect its formal sufficiency; instead, like Hurry
Harry or Tom Hutter, they simply want to break up the picturesque and turn it into property they can sell and profit by. In
other words, nature's beauty has to be protected from tourists and
litterers by a self-proven nobility—a nobility which includes, presumably, someone much like Cooper himself.

In *The Deerslayer*, Cooper sends Natty all the way back to Otsego's savage past to rediscover the timeless ideals of human government and behavior. The young Deerslayer possesses "a window in his breast through which the light of his honesty was ever
shining" and belongs to a better world than that of the later settlements, where people like Richard Jones and Hiram Doolittle
enjoy hiding behind complicated, official words and titles. Deerslayer lives in a world where nature's basic principles of self-
governance are obvious to anyone who pays close enough attention to them, and he guides his life, like Caleb, using truth as his
"polar star" (531). Deerslayer prefers a prelapsarian community
where people respect the value of the words they speak and the
verbal promises they make to others—even to the degree that he
insists on honoring his promise to return to the Mingo camp after
his "furlough," thus surrendering himself to torture and death.
In Deerslayer's world, everyone subscribes to the same common
truths and human principles, just as the Glimmerglass marks the
location of a "common territory" shared by both the warring
Mingoes and Mohicans (14). Even someone as rarely circumspect
as Hurry Harry, one of the most stupidly brutal of Cooper's pioneers (his name signifying the incautious rush of rude men), recognizes that "high principles—modified by habits and prejudices,
but not the less elevated within their circle—can exist in the savage state" (309). Unfortunately, and unlike either Deerslayer or
Chingachgook, Hurry proves himself incapable of actually living
his life according to such principles.

Cooper produces generational sagas rather than novels; for
him, historical or narrative moments always imply eternal landscapes of perfect similitude. Cooper wants to sublimate the dis-

cord of racial and class contradictions into an aesthetic of imperative moral laws. Those who relish conflict or disunity in Cooper's work do so at their own peril. In *The Deerslayer*, the ex-pirate Tom Hutter and the unashamed scalp hunter Hurry Harry consider the wilderness an object they can violate, commodify, and sell; they are incapable of recognizing the larger scope of nature extending beyond the broken scalps and pelts they tear from nature's body. Envisioning the world as a fragmentary collection of things and events which they control, they never realize that nature operates as a perfect continuum of laws and principles which actually controls them.

If people look hard enough, Cooper explains, they can detect meaningful forms and permanent truths in the wilderness the same way readers can imagine idealized landscapes in a book. A moment is not discrete and unitary; it is always implicated in the vaster totality of nature and history. In certain moments, like in certain picturesque landscapes, one can recognize much more than what is merely visible. In *The Deerslayer*, when Tom Hutter, Hurry Harry, Chingachgook, and Wah-ta!-Wah are rowing back to Hutter's "castle" at dawn, they encounter such a "moment" when they notice the mysterious appearance of an Indian moccasin on the castle's wooden platform. There is something about this moment, Cooper suggests, which is both archetypal and sublime. Cooper describes it as the sort of

> moment when everything is distinct, even the atmosphere
> seeming to possess a liquid lucidity, the hues appearing gray
> and softened, with the outlines of objects diffused, and the
> perspective just as moral truths are presented in their sim-
> plicity without the meretricious aids of ornament or glitter.
> In a word, it is the moment when the senses seem to recover
> their powers in the simplest and most accurate forms, like the
> mind emerging from the obscurity of doubts into the tran-
> quility and peace of demonstration. Most of the influence that
> such a scene is apt to produce on those who are properly con-
> stituted in a moral sense was lost on Hutter and Hurry, but
> both the Delawares, though too much accustomed to witness
> the loveliness of morningtide to stop to analyze their feelings,
> were equally sensible of the beauties of the hour, though it
> was probably in a way unknown to themselves. (319)

Because Hurry Harry and Tom Hutter cannot read the complete significance of this moment, they walk blindly into the Mingo ambush; unlike Chingachgook and Wah-ta!-Wah, they lack enough "moral sense" to read the immanent meaning signified by one stray Mingo moccasin. When they are ambushed inside Tom Hutter's "castle," Hutter is scalped in his own home much like a king relieved of his crown, and Hurry is just as abruptly relieved of his inflated pride and self-confidence. Because Hutter and Hurry look at the natural world as a collection of fragments, the world reduces them to fragments in return.

When Deerslayer and Chingachgook return to the Glimmerglass many years after Deerslayer's first transgression (he kills a Mingo in self-defense, but only after that Indian refuses to hear reason and attempts to shoot him in the back), his first act of violence has already been sublimated by nature's seasonal cycle of decay and regeneration. Looking out over the lake at the fallen and moldering "castle," Deerslayer sees that

> the storms of winter had long since unroofed the house, and decay had eaten into the logs. All the fastenings were untouched, but the seasons rioted in the place, as if in mockery at the attempt to exclude them. The palisades were rotting, as were the piles, and it was evident that a few more recurrences of winter, a few more gales and tempests, would sweep all into the lake and blot the building from the face of that magnificent solitude. (532)

Hutter and his family represent everything Cooper thinks a good revolution must overthrow. Hutter himself is a former pirate and scalp hunter who believes he can take things from the wilderness he doesn't deserve; he represents not only the worst attributes of the democratic mob but of the aristocracy as well. As Deerslayer suggests early in the novel, crude pioneers like Hutter act in the wilderness as a sort of proxy gentry. They have moved west in order to secure property for a class of people who don't want to work the property for themselves. When Deerslayer first arrives at the Glimmerglass, he ridicules Hurry for believing that any country this beautiful can "belong" to anybody—either Indian or colonist—and complains about the "gentry" who are "pushing their cravings into the wilderness, even where they never dare to ventur', in their own person, to look at the land they own" (15).

Those who undeservedly inherit their fortunes lack sufficient skills to work property or even appreciate it. Natty hates the "gentry" because they send servants out to get it for them and never work it with their own hands.

Hutter's links to the eastern gentry aren't simply political or commercial, since his deceased wife (whom he has planted at the bottom of the Glimmerglass as a sort of founding mother) was herself a member of that class before she ran away from home.[23] Hutter acts as an agent of aristocratic interests, alienating himself from the natural world around him; similarly, his daughter Judith likes to present herself as a representative of her mother's class, alienating herself from the natural beauty both around and within her. Judith likes to veil her "native beauty" in superficial ornaments and costumes—such as the dress she discovers at the bottom of Hutter's padlocked trunk, one which originally belonged to her mother. Hutter's trunk betrays the secret presence of privileged families in the wilderness, along with Hutter's own role as their effacement. And in the same way Hutter helps disguise the existence of an invisible class of men who aren't around, Judith secretly desires to disguise herself in artificial trappings which disguise her natural, classless beauty—such as when she appears at the Mingo camp to plead for Deerslayer's life, replacing "her ordinary forest attire" with the recovered "brocade" of her dead mother, making the Indians mistakenly assume she is "a woman of rank and importance" (494–495).

Deerslayer, who respects the innate truths and principles of nature while distrusting the slippery, superficial gloss of words, books, and fancy costumes, rejects Judith's marriage proposal for the same reasons he rejects her request that he break his pledge with the Mingoes. Judith is the sort of woman who, like evil Indians or false aristocrats, is constantly tempted to disguise herself with what Deerslayer belittles as mere "colors" and "glitter" (201). Such artificial costumes only disguise her true nature, making her as invisible as the class of people she descends from. To a large extent, Deerslayer is afraid to marry a woman who, unlike nature, doesn't really exist. It isn't surprising, then, that when Judith and Deerslayer dig to the bottom of the Hutter family's trunk they discover a bundle of the deceased Mrs. Hutter's letters from which all the family names have been clipped. The trunk of fantastic, pretentious garments and accoutrements signifies the lapse of name and identity—indicating the absence of a class of men who

don't know how to represent themselves in the wilderness and the
fake "brocade" with which Judith disguises the "natural" woman inside her. As Deerslayer remarks, "Garments make a change to the eye and some change in the conduct, perhaps, but none in the man" (425). Superficial looks and manners do not indicate who someone is but who they are not.

With the fall of the Hutter family "castle" and Judith's own disappearance into history (many years later, Deerslayer hears about a nameless woman in the neighborhood who may or may not be her), only abstractions like history and nature remain. The fall of the Hutter "castle" institutes a kingdom of nature more legitimate than both the democratic pirates who steal land and properties that don't belong to them and the landed gentry who employ them. The fall of the "castle" naturalizes the inheritance of pioneer properties by people who have principles equal to their publicly enunciated names. As Cooper explains in *The Deerslayer*:

> It is well known that little which could be called monarchical or despotic entered into the politics of the North American tribes, although the first colonists, bringing with them to this hemisphere the notions and opinions of their own countries, often dignified the chief men of those primitive nations with the titles of kings and princes. Hereditary influence did certainly exist, but there is much reason to believe it existed rather as a consequence of hereditary merit and acquired qualifications than as a birthright. (475)

The subversion of aristocracy institutes a political order of "natural" merit and acquired hegemony. The Glimmerglass's final lesson is that nature absorbs all political conflict in an embrace which is formal, ahistorical, and purified of specific class or cultural interests; it is simultaneously beautiful and disinterested— like a landscape painting on a wall. Nature, like history (and like the Leatherstocking Saga itself), is that "beautiful gem of the forest" in which everything remains "unchanged" (532). Colonists and revolutionaries do not invade countries and castles; rather, they adopt principles of nature which existed long before castles ever appeared. In order to rule the wilderness, pioneers must not establish new laws but recognize old principles already there— such as, presumably, the Cooper family's rights to determine who observes the spectacular view from Three Mile Point.

Home as Found *and* The Last of the Mohicans:
Revolution, Language, and Difference

*Some changes of the language are to be regretted, as they
lead to false inferences, and society is always a loser by
mistaking names for things. Life is a fact, and it is seldom any
good arises from a misapprehension of the real circumstances
under which we exist. The word "gentleman" has a positive
and limited signification. It means one elevated above the
mass of society by his birth, manners, attainments, character
and social condition. As no civilized society can exist without
these social differences, nothing is gained by denying the use
of the term. If blackguards were to be called "gentlemen,"
and "gentlemen," "blackguards," the difference between
them would be as obvious as it is today.*

—James Fenimore Cooper, *The American Democrat*

*It has often given me pleasure to observe that independent
America was not composed of detached and distant
territories, but that one connected, fertile, wide-spreading
country was the portion of our western sons of liberty.
Providence has in a particular manner blessed it with
a variety of soils and productions and watered it with
innumerable streams for the delight and accommodation of
its inhabitants. A succession of navigable waters forms a kind
of chain round its borders, as if to bind it together; . . .*

*With equal pleasure I have as often taken notice that
Providence has been pleased to give this one connected
country to one united people—a people descended from the
same ancestors, speaking the same language, professing the
same religion, attached to the same principles of government,
very similar in their manners and customs, and who, by
their joint counsels, arms, and efforts, fighting side by side
throughout a long and bloody war, have nobly established
their general liberty and independence.*

*This country and this people seem to have been made for
each other.*

—John Jay, *The Federalist Papers*[24]

In his 1826 preface to *The Last of the Mohicans,* Cooper re-
describes and embellishes his imaginary history of the Delaware-

Mingo conflict. "The greatest difficulty" confronting the student
of this history, he contends, is the "utter confusion that pervades the names," since the colonization of America has systematically retitled Indian lands and translated Indian titles.[25] For Cooper, both revolution and imperialism are noted by their "effort to subvert things by names" (*The American Democrat*, 174). In his retelling of the Indian wars, Cooper recalls an original native purity which existed long before pioneers and revolutionaries came along to corrupt language and meaning.

The Europeans, Cooper continues in his preface, "found that immense region which lies between the Penobscot and the Potomac, the Atlantic and the Mississippi, in the possession of a people who sprang from the same stock" (2). Property was unified by the racial purity and integrity of its "people." As Cooper goes on to explain:

> The generic name of this people was the Wapanachki. They were fond, however, of calling themselves the "Lenni Lenape," which of itself signifies, an "unmixed people." It would far exceed the information of the author, to enumerate a moiety of the communities, or tribes, into which this race of beings was subdivided. Each tribe had its name, its chiefs, its hunting grounds, and, frequently, its dialect. Like the feudal princes of the old world, they fought among themselves, and exercised most of the other privileges of sovereignty. Still, they admitted the claims of a common origin, a similar language, and of that moral interest, which was so faithfully and so wonderfully transmitted through their traditions. . . .
> The tribe that possessed the country which now composes the south-western parts of New-England, and that portion of New-York that lies east of the Hudson, and the country even much farther to the south, was a mighty people, called the "Mahicanni," or, more commonly, the "Mohicans." The latter word has since been corrupted by the English, into "Mohegan." (2)

Cooper compares this original "unmixed people" with the "feudal princes" of old Europe, who, despite competing dialects and territories, shared a common familial identity. Two things threaten this original Indian aristocracy, however: European colonists and the highly fragmented tribes of Mingoes who mix freely with Dutch and French settlers. These Mingoes surge with primitive violence; they are "less united" than the Lenni Lenape because they have preserved neither the purity of their race nor the integrity of their language.

As Dennis W. Allen and Steven Blakemore have argued, the Mohicans' war with the satanic Hurons describes a conflict between pre- and postlapsarian cultures.[26] The Mohicans are not simply racially pure but the original proprietors of "the eastern and northern states of America." Their hegemony is challenged by European languages, which corrupt the integrity of ancestral Mohican names. European invasion "sever[s] in many places" the "great tie of language, and, of course, of a common origin" (197). Language is a fabric knitted from an original racial cloth; it remains intact only so long as its racial integrity prevails. European colonialism violates not only Indian properties but both their language and their racial identity. The Mohicans are "corrupted by the English" into Mohegan in an act of colonial violence, just as the Mingoes are "mislabeled" Iroquois and Lake Horican is renamed Lake George.[27]

Like the early Indian language scholar Duponceau, Cooper argues that native American language originally possessed an Edenic, prelapsarian integrity. As Steven Blakemore explains, the "Indian word is part of a particular contextual world, and its connection with the body metaphorically makes the world flesh. As the Indian word is bodied forth in the blood and bone of its contextual world, the suggestive result is a language that is physically clear and as palpable as the body."[28] Indian language embodies the very breath and muscle of a race. As Natty explains to Chingachgook, a European mistakenly learns "the names of black marks" rather than the spoken "deeds of his fathers" (31). Spoken language invests individuals with the physical integrity of their race; written language severs things from names and properties from legal titles. Instead of reading words in books, people should recall the acts of their parents and the integrity of their families.

The unremitting violence of *Mohicans* describes a revolution of words over things which, uncontrolled by laws or principles, escalates into increasingly mad, undifferentiated violence.[29] Like Satan, Magua's power lies in his ability to deceive; he corrupts his own language with French (the language Cooper associates with the violent excesses of Enlightenment philosophy) just as he seeks to disguise the world's truth behind an artificial "supplement" of false signs. Magua, like Hutter and Harry or even Judith, wants to make nature into things it isn't—false trails, political subterfuge, and broken vows. While Magua wields his deceptive signs, Natty and the Mohicans seek to identify and reunify those signs with the wilderness's vaster symbolic meaning. Natty and the Mohicans want to reunite language and the world; they want to reassign identity to the world's body by unraveling Magua's fake clues and false trails, erasing his mistranslations and correcting his deliberate errata.

Natty explains to David Gamut that he has little faith in "books," preferring to read the face of nature instead. Books multiply words rather than attach them to their original meanings; Natty disregards this literary multiplicity by reading nowhere but in the "one" true book of Nature. "The words that are written there," he claims, "are too simple and too plain to need much schooling" (117). These are words which do not require trained minds, for they elicit a natural, instinctive sympathy from any person who possesses what Cooper refers to in *The Deerslayer* as a "moral sense." In *Mohicans*, Natty continues:

> "I have heard it said, that there are men who read in books, to convince themselves there is a God! I know not but man may so deform his works in the settlements, as to leave that which is so clear in the wilderness, a matter of doubt among traders and priests. If any such there be, and he will follow me from sun to sun, through the windings of the forest, he shall see enough to teach him that he is a fool, and that the greatest of his folly lies in striving to rise to the level of one he can never equal, be it in goodness, or be it in power." (117)

Experienced fully, the wilderness reveals the "magnificent solitude" of God that words cannot convey. There is a point where people must look beyond words and into the world.

For Cooper, a world gone mad is a world ruled by fallen language, where the names and appearances of things are constantly shifting and changing, like Magua's wilderness trails or the radical reassignment of property titles demanded by Anti-Renters. Uncas proves his true nobility by being able to "read" through false or misleading signs; at one point, he is called upon to explicate an enemy scalp, like some professor enlisted to scan a rhyme. As Natty informs Duncan Heyward:

> "Now, to white eyes there is no difference between this bit of skin and that of any other Indian, and yet the Sagamore de-

clares it came from the poll of a Mingo; nay, he even names the tribe of the poor devil, with as much ease as if the scalp was the leaf of a book, and each hair a letter. What right have christian whites to boast of their learning, when a savage can read a language, that would prove too much for the wisest of them all!" (196)

Indians recognize in language and nature a system of perfect synecdoche; in fragments they can read the stories of entire races, nations, geographies, continents. By reading a single object Uncas apprehends an entire world; meanwhile, Magua (like Hutter and Hurry Harry) attempts to break that world into inarticulate fragments. Reading, like Emerson's reason, ideally penetrates objects and discloses a "more earnest vision" of them. To anyone who employs this "vision," "outlines and surfaces become transparent, and are no longer seen; causes and spirits are seen through them."[30] Magua, however, like Godwin's aristocrats, wants to throw a veil over the world and reduce it to a blizzard of superficial appearances disconnected from any true meaning.

The pursuit of Magua leads Hawkeye and his companions from the slaughter at Fort Henry into an increasingly discontinuous wilderness of broken language.[31] While Magua systematically distorts nature, Natty and the Mohicans, "three of the best pair of eyes on the borders," penetrate Magua's secret trails by reattaching significance to the deceptive signs Magua leaves behind, journeying across the "broken" landscape "with as much confidence as a traveller would proceed along a wide highway. If a rock, or a rivulet, or a bit of earth harder than common, severed the links of the clue they followed, the true eye of the scout recovered them at a distance, and seldom rendered the delay of a single moment necessary" (214).

Magua's deceptions would easily "blind white eyes," Natty insists, because whites trust mere words—words such as those in their multitudinous books. As the chase progresses, Duncan Heyward serves as a sort of reading foil to Natty, always misunderstanding the true meaning of signs: mistaking a dam for a cataract, beasts for Indians, a beaver pond for a lake. Cooper claims that Heyward's ability to misread can be "better imagine[d]" by the reader than described, since his readers, Cooper implies, are supposedly good ones (perhaps simply because they have chosen to read Cooper). Good readers extrapolate from individual signs

to imagine entire situations; unlike poor Heyward, they never accept words in themselves—black markings on white paper, or the
sound of vowels and consonants in the mouth. Words, read correctly, indicate the world's fullness. To the intelligent reader nature presents what Natty calls "infallible signs"; by learning to
read nature properly, people can live in perfect relation with it,
like the Indian who "rests secure under his knowledge of the signs
of the forest, and the long and difficult paths that separate him
from those he has most reason to dread" (232). Signs lead people
down correct paths; language is a means of traveling, exploring,
colonizing those dark spaces one would otherwise avoid. Signs
make the world exploitable as well as known.

By disrupting the significations of things, Magua creates a
world of false appearances that allows Natty and his companions
(disguised by now as other men and wild animals) to invade the
Mingo camp. Natty's long progress through the violent, corrupted
landscape of Magua leads him not into greater disorder but back
to the most primitive embodiment of tribal law. In order to resolve their conflict with Magua, Natty and the Mohicans appeal
to the judgment of ancient Tamenund, whose body is adorned with
the emblems of both kingly power and natural merit:

> His bosom was loaded with medals, some in massive silver,
> and one or two even in gold, the gifts of various christian po-
> tentates, during the long period of his life. He also wore arm-
> lets, and cinctures above the ancles, of the latter precious
> metal. His head, on the whole of which the hair had been per-
> mitted to grow, the pursuits of war having so long been aban-
> doned, was encircled by a sort of plated diadem, which, in its
> turn, bore lesser and more glittering ornaments, that sparkled
> amid the glossy hues of three drooping ostrich feathers, dyed a
> deep black, in touching contrast to the colour of his snow-
> white locks. His tomahawk was nearly hid in silver, and the
> handle of his knife shone like a horn of solid gold. (293)

As usual in Cooper, superficial signs of authority mark the location
of authority's absence; it is as if the king's accoutrements simply
designate another deceptive space in an undependable world—
like Natty's disguise as a bear or Chingachgook's wolf impression.
Tamenund's pretentious "dignity of a monarch" does not identify
the place of authority, only its displacement, indicating a power

that resides not in Tamenund himself but somewhere else entirely (294). Roused by Tamenund's imposture, Uncas reveals himself "in front of the nation with the air of a king" (309). Near the end of *Mohicans*, Uncas no longer searches through the wilderness's trail of broken signifiers; instead, he himself manifests the ultimate signified. Unadorned by medals and gold, he reveals upon his chest one primordial hieroglyph: the image of an enormous turtle carrying the entire world upon its back. It is a symbol which does not fragment or obscure authority but unifies it with the king's body. Uncas does not simply wear a costume of authority which, like Tamenund's, can be exchanged from one man to another; instead, he embodies law, authority, and racial purity. Recalling the original authority of the Indian races through the naked display of his own body, Uncas's subsequent call to pursue Magua and Cora reawakens "all the slumbering passions of the nation" (320).

Uncas's death, like Major Effingham's symbolic resurrection, legitimates the white appropriation (or "inheritance") of Indian property according to white European law. Colonists do not steal the land but inherit it from the last true king, from the very source of the wilderness who, like the turtle, carries the entire world of nature on its back. Colonists do not impose false names or deeds on the land but reveal true names and titles, just as revolutionaries do not impose arbitrary false laws but divulge eternal ones.

In his later work, Cooper increasingly worries about American property becoming corrupted by floods of European immigrants during the thirties and forties. While radical democratic rhetoric describes property as a surplus which must be perpetually redistributed, Cooper becomes obsessed with assigning property to a permanent class of owners. The more insecure Cooper becomes, the farther he retreats into the past, gathering historical weight into his sagas of Leatherstocking and the Effinghams in order to define geographical boundaries as both implicitly personal and historically concrete. While democratic agitation seeks to break up existing patroonships and redistribute them, Cooper defends the legitimate tenures of America's "natural" aristocrats. According to him, an exemplary family's property at once shapes, and is shaped by, the family name; name and object, then, become interpenetrated, absolute, and permanently fixed. Anti-Renters, on the other hand (much like the "speculators" Judge Temple disdains), seek to corrupt both property and language by imposing false, transient names on properties that don't belong to them.

In *Home as Found*, Cooper's ideal "natural" aristocrat, Mr. Effingham, confronts the democratic spokesman, Mr. Bragg, who demands that all political differences and distinctions between citizens be eliminated. By erasing permanent distinctions, Mr. Bragg and the democratic rabble threaten to make all words the same; they want to make a "blackguard" of a "gentleman" and a "gentleman" of a "blackguard." While Mr. Bragg respects the "regular movers" who never develop stable residences, John Effingham prefers the British aristocrats like Sir George Templemore who "love to continue for generations on the same spot."[32] Like Templeton's yeoman farmers, aristocrats want to live beside the trees that their "forefathers planted, the roof that they built, the fireside by which they sat, the sods that cover their remains" (23). Natural aristocrats want to make their families and land into one permanent estate; they want to make title and property indivisible.

Mr. Bragg, on the other hand, prefers a world in which names and properties can be easily disconnected; his ideal capitalist world is filled with transformative values and fluctuating exchange rates. Mr. Bragg believes that America has quite correctly dispensed with everything "in the way of history," since anything fixed, like memory or tradition, is restrictive and dull. He even goes so far as to argue that a "nation is much to be pitied that is weighed down by the past, in this manner, since its industry and enterprise are constantly impeded by obstacles that grow out of its recollections" (23). America should not enforce tradition but break from it; historical or familial associations impede the progressive acquisition and development of new properties, enterprises, expenditures, and profits. John Effingham, however, condemns any such "business" which disregards "the recollections of ancestry" (23). By arguing that property titles should be arbitrarily assigned according to that "paper currency" which Cooper rigorously disparages in his novels, Mr. Bragg threatens to create a world of ruptured signification as anarchic as Magua's roving bands of freelance Iroquois.[33]

For Cooper, family title disciplines property and yokes it to proper names, while the "permanent revolution" of capitalist exchange values continuously invalidates signification. John Effingham distrusts the democratic tendency "to love change" because it disrupts identity, hegemony, and order. As he warns the baronet:

> "Take Templeton, for instance; this little place has not essentially increased in numbers within my memory, and yet fully one half its names are new. When he reaches his own home, your father will not know even the names of one half his neighbors. Not only will he meet with new faces, but he will find new feelings, new opinions in the place of traditions that he may love, an indifference to everything but the present moment, and even those who may have better feelings, and a wish to cherish all that belongs to the holier sentiments of man, afraid to utter them lest they meet with no sympathy." (118)

Radical, unchecked democracy makes reality, property, and truth into transient, indeterminate propositions. By allowing the names of properties and people to become interchangeable, democracy exposes people of firm temperament and abilities to "new feelings" and "new opinions" which contradict European traditions without strengthening or improving them.

The "real American gentleman," Eve Effingham asserts, can never "be the inferior of an English baronet" so long as he maintains the integrity of his property. John Effingham refuses to abandon his home because he wants to maintain his inherited status. Rather than dismantle the American past embodied by his home, the Wigwam, Effingham improves upon its original design, which was left to him by his "great predecessor," Natty Bumppo (114). The Effinghams have not simply "inherited" Indian property but Indian names; the Wigwam is passed down to their family by that same white man who first managed to forge a symbolic kinship with the Indian race. Natty, the "man without a cross," represents that "natural" man through whom Indian property can be translated into white culture without the races themselves ever intersecting. Natty, the original transgressor of Templeton's laws and land, becomes institutionalized within the body of Effingham's estate, and Effingham himself refers to him as an equal of George Washington, for together they are "the two only really great men of my time" (200). Effingham's vision of the American hero as a combination revolutionary soldier and wilderness pathfinder conflates the colonial "father" with the natural aristocrat, just as colonial names (such as Wigwam) conflate Indian names with white properties.

Despite Natty's great skill "with the spear as with the rifle," he
is remembered as a man who has been unable to catch "sight of the sogdollager" (200), which breathes and drifts at the bottom of Lake Otsego like a sort of miniature whale—irreproachable, ageless, and titanic with significance. The dark realm of the sogdollager describes the final zone of untransgressable authority, always hidden by and deferred to a place more monumental than history. As the commodore explains to Eve:

> "A sogdollager, young lady, is the perfection of a thing. I know Mr. Grant used to say there was no such word in the dictionary; but then there are many words that ought to be in the dictionaries that have been forgotten by the printers. In the way of salmon trout, the sogdollager is their commodore. Now, ladies and gentlemen, I should not like to tell you all I know about the patriarch of the lake, for you would scarcely believe me; but if he would not weigh a hundred when cleaned, there is not an ox in the county that will weigh a pound when slaughtered." (198–199)

Men can never catch or kill the sogdollager, the commodore explains; they can only hope to glimpse it beneath the lake's glimmering surface. Having himself once managed to catch sight of the sogdollager's gills, the commodore had felt like Washington "the night Cornwallis surrendered" (199).

Just as parliamentary democracy "re-presents" citizens by subordinating them to a central authority, democratically natural men are always represented in Cooper's novels by individual characters such as Oliver, John Effingham, Natty, and Uncas. In his essay "American and European Scenery Compared," Cooper acknowledges:

> To conclude, we concede to Europe much the noblest scenery . . . in all those effects which depend on time and association, in its monuments, and in this impress of the past which may be said to be reflected in its countenance; while we claim for America the freshness of a most promising youth, and a species of natural radiance that carries the mind with reverence to the source of all that is glorious around us.[34]

Cooper distinguishes Europe and America as two different realms of nature; Europe's respect for past traditions and binding "associations" juxtaposes American unfamiliarity and "freshness." The

American "break" with European scenery describes a more divine apprehension of "all that is glorious," proving Americans
superior to the Old World's class-conscious bureaucrats. Aristocratic authority can never be "naturalized" so much as deferred
beyond nature's border: that always limitless space where everything is invested by everything, the imaginary realm of nature,
history, the sublime, the West. Revolution translates the body of
the aristocrat into a symbol of everything the aristocrat is not:
Everybody.

Edgar Allan Poe
and the
Exaltation of Form

The Wreck of the Grampus:
Recovering Original Violence in
The Narrative of Arthur Gordon Pym

It is not in the power of any mere worldly
considerations, such as these, to depress
me . . . No, my sadness is *unaccountable, and*
this makes me the more sad. I am full of dark
forebodings.

> —Edgar Allan Poe,
>   letter to Annie L. Richmond[1]

The pen which wrote Caleb Williams, should
never for a moment be idle.

> —Edgar Allan Poe, reviewing
>   Godwin's *Lives of the Necromancers*[2]

Poe died calling out for Reynolds, dreaming, like most nineteenth-century Americans, of the infinite possibilities of a limitless frontier. Thirteen years earlier, in an essay published in the same issue of the *Southern Literary Messenger* as the first installment of *The Narrative of Arthur Gordon Pym*, Poe praised J. N. Reynolds's plans to map commercial routes in the Pacific and South Seas because they would contribute to the formation of "that main prop of our national power,—a hardy, effective, and well disciplined national navy."[3] For Poe, Reynolds's expedition would fulfill America's dream of unlimited exploitation by establishing military integrity. By providing "fuel" for "America's developing economy," the South Seas would help America achieve manifest destiny by constantly becoming more than it already was.

Reynolds's projected enterprise causes Poe to reflect on whether "the Rocky Mountains shall forever constitute the western boundary of our republic, or that it shall not stretch its dominion from sea to sea" (1231). In his reverie of manifest destiny, Poe reveals his affinity with Godwinian rationalism in his belief that by penetrating surfaces and spaces, men and women achieve their fundamental human purpose. One should never "set limits to knowledge," Poe explains, for so "long as there is mind to act upon matter, the realms of science must be enlarged; and nature and her laws be better understood, and more understandingly applied to the great purpose of life" (1242). Poe goes on to suggest that people explore the world in order

> to collect, preserve, and arrange every thing valuable in the whole range of natural history, from the minute madrapore to the huge spermaceti, and accurately to describe that which cannot be preserved; to secure whatever may be hoped for in natural philosophy; to examine vegetation, from the hundred mosses of the rocks, throughout all the classes of shrub, flower and tree, up to the monarch of the forest; to study man in his physical and mental powers, in his manners, habits, disposition, and social and political relations; and above all, in the philosophy of his language, in order to trace his origin from the early families of the old world . . . in fine, there should be science enough to bear upon every thing that may present itself for investigation. (1243)

For Poe, the acquisition of knowledge leads Man to discover the "trace of his origin." By venturing into unknown worlds, men recall the "early families of the old world" they left behind. Ex-

ploration simultaneously discovers the unknown and preserves
the known—whether it be the "huge spermaceti" or America's
own European ancestry. By transgressing the frontier, Americans
catalog and preserve their own various "social and political relations," achieving immortality by writing memories of themselves
in a book. What the world ultimately teaches Americans is that
they, like everything else, must perish. Their written memory of
themselves, on the other hand, will last forever.

Proponents of unlimited western expansion dreamed of
Symmes's hollow earth just as Poe dreamed of an essentially hollow reality. By journeying beyond the horizon of the known, explorers could discover a new world at the exact same moment
they vanished forever from this one. In "Ms. Found in a Bottle,"
a story directly prefiguring *Pym*, the doomed narrator envisions
himself and his dead crew "hurrying onwards to some exciting
knowledge—some never-to-be-imparted secret, whose attainment
is destruction."[4] Like Godwin's Caleb, Poe's characters seek to
penetrate geographic limits and disclose universal secrets; but by
disclosing these secrets, Poe's characters simultaneously vanish
into them. Poe's dream of unlimited westward expansion is simultaneously a nightmare as well. While Godwin believes that
exploration leads to improving humanity and knowledge, Poe believes it leads to nothing but destruction.[5]

A furious reactionary, Poe opposes the principles of bourgeois
revolution not simply because they undermine aristocratic government but because they impede colonial progress. For Poe,
revolution acts "as a temporary check" to the economic exploitation of the Pacific (1228), and his novel, *The Narrative of Arthur Gordon Pym*, describes revolution as the ultimate threat to
imperial expansion. Poe dreams of the frontier as a region of in-
surrection and chaos, madness and death. Where Godwin envisions reason as an instrument which we employ to understand
the world around and within us, Poe ironizes the reason of common citizens as a sort of pretension. In Poe's universe, people only
presume to understand the world; meanwhile, the world relentlessly tears them apart along with everything else.[6]

Like both *Caleb Williams* and *Edgar Huntly*, Poe's novel can be
divided into two parts.[7] The first half describes class conflict in
psychological terms, while the second half extends this conflict
geographically. In Poe's novel, however, the revelation of "natu-

ral Man" always reveals a scene of monstrous violence and catas-
trophe. Poe believes that human "nature" is redemptive only in
the most ironic and brutal sense; if "natural Man" serves a purpose in Poe's universe, it is to destroy himself.

Naive, restless, and enthusiastic, Arthur Pym prefers the shadowy world of "art" to the rocky, mundane world of reality; he
prefers the stories and adventures his friend Augustus reads to
him at night to the dull routines of his job and family. As a result,
Arthur never explores the world so much as imagines it. Drifting
in the reveries of bedtime tales and nightmarish visions, buried
beneath the surfaces of ships and continents, Arthur invents the
world far more often than he ever experiences it.[8] Arthur isn't
interested in either wealth or knowledge so much as tempted by
aesthetic intensity. Long before Arthur realizes that Augustus's
youthful tales of high adventure are "sheer fabrications," he already envisions the world beyond his artistically imposed town
of "Edgarton" as a fabrication itself or a sort of lustrous and hy-
perimaginary painting. As Pym explains:

> For the bright side of the painting I had a limited sympathy.
> My visions were of shipwreck and famine; of death or captiv-
> ity among barbarian hordes; of a lifetime dragged out in sor-
> row and tears, upon some gray and desolate rock, in an ocean
> unapproachable and unknown. Such visions or desires—for
> they amounted to desires—are common, I have since been as-
> sured, to the whole numerous race of the melancholy among
> men—at the time of which I speak I regarded them only as
> prophetic glimpses of a destiny which I felt myself in a mea-
> sure bound to fulfill.[9]

Pym, like many of Poe's "melancholiacs," feels a deep, cellular
dissatisfaction with the world's "bright side," preferring the shadowy world of "sorrow and tears." For him, destiny is filled with a
sense of loss and mourning; by achieving it, he loses everything,
including himself.

Arthur's melancholy makes him feel detached from the transitory world and unresponsive to its authority.[10] When Arthur's parents object to his proposed sea adventure with Augustus and Captain Barnard, Arthur quickly resorts to deception and disguise,
abilities by which he feels he "can accomplish wonders" (56). By
"appearing" to accept the "design" of his parents, Arthur takes a

certain pride in his hypocrisy, which is "rendered tolerable" to
him "by the wild and burning expectation" he feels whenever he
anticipates the "fulfillment" of his "long-cherished visions of
travel" (58). Pym readily adopts fictive identities because his notion of travel is itself fictive, a poetic journey into regions of both
"vision" and "painting." Even after his first preliminary adventure
in which he and Augustus are lost at sea and nearly drowned,
Arthur's enthusiasm remains undiminished; in fact, his experiences of shipwreck and near-drowning only teach him to more
fully appreciate the wild world's "picturesqueness" and its "exciting points of color" (57).

Arthur adopts concealments as steadfastly as Caleb penetrates
them.[11] He uses forged letters to flee his family, as well as a "thick
seaman's cloak" and affected accent to evade his curious uncle.
He does not dread the prison's impenetrable darkness so much as
seek it out; when Augustus leads him into his covert den underneath the brig of the *Grampus*, Arthur recounts that "I proceeded
immediately to take possession of my little apartment, and this
with feelings of higher satisfaction, I am sure, than any monarch
ever experienced upon entering a new palace" (62). Arthur's iden-
tification of his secret tomb with a monarchical estate is not entirely facetious. For Poe, both orphaned and estranged from his
wealthy stepfather, social privilege could never be attained except as nostalgic reverie. By recalling his privileged life, Poe must
simultaneously recall his loss of it; as a result, he was the perfect
poet to recognize postrevolutionary aristocratic power as a dream
of the already vanquished and the dead.

Immured within his secret kingdom, Arthur learns how quickly
the king's palace can become a mausoleum—as quickly as corpses
decay and food spoils. The cold mutton which he finds "excellent" before falling asleep suddenly turns, upon his awakening,
to "a state of absolute putrefaction" (64). As the physical com-
forts of his kingdom quickly grow cold and damp and his supplies
diminish, Arthur retreats into the same catastrophic dreaming
which elicited his tragic adventuring in the first place:

> My dreams were of the most terrific description. Every species
> of calamity and horror befell me. Among other miseries, I was
> smothered to death between huge pillows, by demons of the
> most ghastly and ferocious aspect. Immense serpents held me
> in their embrace, and looked earnestly in my face with their

fearfully shining eyes. Then deserts, limitless, and of the most forlorn and awe-inspiring character, spread themselves out before me. Immensely tall trunks of trees, gray and leafless, rose up in endless succession as far as the eye could reach. Their roots were concealed in wide-spreading morasses, whose dreary water lay intensely black, still, and altogether terrible, beneath. And the strange trees seemed endowed with a human vitality, and, waving to and fro their skeleton arms, were crying to the silent waters for mercy, in the shrill and piercing accents of the most acute agony and despair. (65–66)

Pym dreams of penetrating the world, but only to divulge madness, cannibalism, suffering, and death. The natural world is not only filled with dangerous creatures—snakes and lions and demons—but with the terrible brutalities of all-too-natural men. Nature is that black tangled morass in which men, like trees, are deeply rooted. Pym's dream is filled with terrible cries, just as he fills the world with his own cries upon awakening—the cry of men trapped by the very world they originally presumed to conquer. This cry of men and beasts resembles the "thunder of the firmament" and is, in fact, both heaven's divine utterance and its fisted retribution; it is the cry of pain which enunciates the victim's horrible desires for redemption and revenge (66).

Poe's aversion to democratic Federalism, as well as his fervent support of slavery, arises from his fundamental belief that people are radically unequal; as he explains in one of his "Marginalia," northern Federalists, like the European bourgeoisie, mistakenly locate human "reason" in nature. Such "theorizers on Government," Poe contends,

who pretend always to "begin with the beginning," commence with Man in what they call his *natural* state—the savage. What right have they to suppose this his natural state? Man's chief idiosyncrasy being reason, it follows that his savage condition—his condition of action *without* reason—is his *un*natural state. The more he reasons, the nearer he approaches the position to which this chief idiosyncrasy irresistibly impels him; and not until he attains this position with exactitude—not until his reason has exhausted itself for his improvement—not until he has stepped upon the highest pinnacle of civilisation—will his *natural* state be ultimately reached, or thoroughly determined.[12]

True reason is something few attain to escape their "natural
state" of brute ignorance. Poe distinguishes here between Man's
"natural state in the world" and Man's "natural state beyond this
world," implying that in the latter one enjoys perfect harmony
with the vast pulse and hum of a pure, Godlike intelligence. For
Poe, Man's natural state *in the world* (where men appear reasonable only by disguising their unreasoning nature) is always hor-
rific. In his first seafaring adventure with Augustus, Pym mistakenly assumes that Augustus is in control of both the ship and his
own senses, but he soon recognizes Augustus's "highly concen-
trated state of intoxication—a state which, like madness, frequently enables the victim to imitate the outward demeanor of
one in perfect possession of his senses" (50). Those who appear
reasonable usually disguise the deepest kind of madness. And the
lesson Pym keeps learning over and over again is that madness,
rather than reason, is the only natural attribute everybody shares.

If even Augustus (Pym's "rational" side, as some critics have
argued) can disguise his inherent senselessness, then an insane
world can also disguise itself as rational and orderly—but only
for so long.[13] Mutiny on board the *Grampus* occurs spontaneously—at that very moment, in fact, when Augustus decides to
continue deceiving his father, Captain Barnard, about Pym's hidden presence under the floorboards. The mutineers are not concerned with making rational political changes in the ship's hierarchy, nor are they motivated "for the sake of booty"; rather, they
are gratuitously provoked by "a private pique of the chief mate's
against Captain Barnard" (93). According to Poe, mutiny arises
from basic human perversity and not as a response to specific political situations. This "private pique" between two men quickly
escalates into a series of increasingly violent confrontations, finally "releasing" the black cook from that class and racial hierarchy which formerly kept him in his place. The cook (and, in
fact, "blackness" itself) represents transgression incarnate. After
the mutiny succeeds, the first mate entreats the cook for mercy,
but the cook's "only reply" is "a blow on the forehead from an
axe" (83). The cook single-handedly murders twenty-two of the
crew by "striking each victim on the head," asserting a radical
democracy of undifferentiated violence without any regard for
distinctions of individual character or importance (84).

The mutiny never achieves a new leader or government but
only a sort of primal lawlessness, a leaderless world of the ruth-

lessly "equal" and "free." The mutineers continue to suffer "frequent and violent quarrels among themselves, in one of which a harpooner, Jim Bonner, was thrown overboard," and when a drunken member of the cook's gang also falls overboard he drowns in front of the eyes of his companions, with "no attempt being made to save him" (104). After their various mutinies—against parents, captain, law, and nature—everyone in this novel (much like the skeletal trees in Pym's feverish dream) ends up equally mired in death, destruction, and the sea. When the cook binds and imprisons Augustus in the forecastle, he warns him that "he will never put his foot on deck again 'until the brig was no longer a brig.' This was the expression of the cook, who threw him into the berth—it is hardly possible to say what precise meaning was intended by the phrase" (88). The cook wants to disregard the proper names of things, tossing overboard the nautical distinctions of ships along with their legal owners. His phrase itself lacks any "precise meaning," making of language the same gibberish his axe makes of political order. The mutineers presume to create a better government by murdering the crew, but the violence of revolution returns again and again, like repressed guilt in modernist psychology.[14]

In a world without clear differences, the line between real and unreal dissolves; it becomes impossible to distinguish between the apparent and the actual. Long before Pym disguises himself as a zombie, the crew's "superstitious terrors and guilty conscience" have already prepared them to believe in the resurrection of the dead. With their pistols and muskets still lying randomly about, the crew is readily "contrived" by Peters "to turn the conversation upon the bloody deeds of the mutiny, and by degrees [to] talk of the thousand superstitions which are so universally current among seamen" (115). The crew are not frightened by apparent ghosts or monsters so much as by their own unreason. In Arthur's masquerade they confront the supernatural forces of their own rebellion; they believe the world is as mad as they are. As Arthur explains:

> It is not too much to say that such remnants of doubt have
> been at the bottom of almost every such visitation, and that
> the appalling horror which has sometimes been brought
> about, is to be attributed, even in the cases most in point, and
> where most suffering has been experienced, more to a kind of

anticipative horror, lest the apparition *might possibly be* real, than to an unwavering belief in its reality. (116)

Men do not fear what they know so much as what they don't understand: mutiny, storms, discord, dynamite, hunger, and thirst. They fear a world of nature more terrible and unimaginable than nightmares.

The real world quickly proves how terrible it can be: after the mutineers flee Arthur's fake apparition and dive overboard, a storm wrecks the *Grampus* and Arthur and his fellow survivors cling to the flotsam; they get drunk, go crazy, eat each other, and forlornly hope for salvation. When a Dutch brig approaches in the distance, Arthur makes the same mistake he has been making all along: he keeps thinking things will get better. The lesson of the Dutch brig, as J. Gerald Kennedy convincingly demonstrates, teaches Arthur and his fellow survivors that any promise of rescue or redemption always "reveals itself as a ghastly emblem of their corporeal fate."[15] Even when the Dutch brig first appears, Arthur finds himself so awestruck that he is "unable to articulate a syllable" (130). Because of the brig's disinterested approach, Arthur immediately suspects "the helmsman to be in liquor," causing him to reflect yet again on the duplicities of worldly appearances and human character. Eventually, however, he distinguishes the three seamen:

> Two of these were lying on some old sails near the forecastle, and the third, who appeared to be looking at us with great curiosity, was leaning over the starboard bow near the bowsprit. This last was a stout and tall man, with a very dark skin. He seemed by his manner to be encouraging us to have patience, nodding to us in a cheerful although rather odd way, and smiling constantly, so as to display a set of the most brilliantly white teeth . . . I relate these things and circumstances minutely, and I relate them, it must be understood, precisely as they *appeared* to us. (131)

As if mocking Pym's attempts to examine and "relate" "circumstances" in his ponderous diary entries, the "tall" seaman "appears" to be a sort of paradigmatically benign bourgeois figure, displaying Caleb's healthy curiosity, peering confidently into the world. Upon closer examination, however, Poe's Enlightenment figure proves to be no more than a corpse staring into nothingness

Edgar Allan Poe

while birds devour his flesh. While men pretend to penetrate the world, the world busily penetrates them.

Pym, like many of Poe's characters, consistently proves himself less perceptive than the author who created him, continually expressing doubts about his literary adequacy; meanwhile, hidden among *Pym*'s linguistic folds like a spider, Poe designs a malicious fiction that pretends to be factual narrative, while that factual narrative pretends to be fiction (if only to be believed). In his preface, Arthur explains that initially he tried to write "from mere memory, a statement so minute and connected as to have the *appearance* of that truth it would really possess" (43). But doubting his own abilities to convince readers of the truth, he nearly gave up the project until the intercession of "Mr. Poe," who convinced him that if he published his account "*under the garb of fiction*," its very "uncouthness" and lack of authorial polish would convince readers of his veracity. Poe is not simply creating a Derridean play of signification, forcing his readers to unravel the metaphysical complicities of fact and fiction; he is ridiculing the ability of readers to tell the difference between truth and illusion, meaning and madness. The problem is not in language itself, Poe believes, but in the faulty, too-human people who try to read it. The punch line of Poe's preamble arrives at the public's expense, since anyone who trusts in their own "shrewdness and common sense" has come to believe in the literal existence of a character who vanishes into his own narrative (44). Any reader who presumes to possess enough "common sense" to differentiate fact from fiction will, like Pym himself, stupidly identify fiction as fact, death as life, and doom as salvation.

Throughout his career, Poe delighted in hoaxing common readers. By believing in the vulgar referentiality of fake news articles and fictions disguised as fact, the democratic mob proved itself incapable of appreciating that "indefiniteness" of poetry which Poe glorified in his critical essays. It is only by means of this poetic "indefiniteness" that true authors, as well as their more sensitive readers, can successfully flee the doomed world— an ability which, as Charles Feidelson, Jr., describes it, exemplifies the artist's "power to transcend the finite words of the mob." [16] As Evelyn J. Hinz has argued, Pym's attempts to describe or catalog the world are always ironized, since no matter how much scientific authority Pym pretends to possess, he is routinely enveloped by unreasonable events and inexplicit terrors. [17] In con-

cluding his preface, Pym claims it isn't really necessary for him
to inform the public which portions of his narrative are written by his editor, Poe, and which are written by himself, for "the difference in point of style will be readily perceived" (45). By this point, Poe's contempt for his "hoaxed" readers is clearly audible.

Arthur is not only a bad writer but a bad reader as well. The smile which urges Arthur "on to hope" belongs to a skeleton who peers as intently at the shipwreck survivors as Arthur, in his scientific journals, peers at the natural world (133). Pym's desire to make sense of the world only leads him farther into its senselessness; he is always much better at imagining worldly salvation than at achieving it. As Arthur recounts, even when he and his fellow survivors "plainly saw that not a soul lived in that fated vessel," still they could not prevent themselves from "shouting to the dead for help" (132). Throughout the *Narrative*, Poe's protagonist cries out "to the dead for help" only to realize, again and again, that his own corporeality already places him among their numbers.

When the carnivorous seagull drops the "curious" seaman's bloody eyeball into Arthur's lap, Arthur instinctively feels an unmentionable desire to devour it himself. The scenes of madness and cannibalism which follow are all made plausible by this "instinctive" response, since it suggests that cannibalism is an innately "natural" human capacity just waiting for an opportunity to get out. Even on the shipwrecked *Grampus* the castaways find ways to get drunk (selfishly, of course, and at Pym's expense), and once drinking releases their inner natures, the castaways all suffer a similarly monstrous "distortion of countenance" (137). Eventually the mutiny's few survivors battle amongst themselves, madly and bloodily devouring the same Parker who had sought to devour Pym, while Pym himself feels toward his "poor fellow creature, Parker, the most intense, the most diabolic hatred" (145).

"Such things may be imagined," Pym explains, after recounting Parker's slaughter, "but words have no power to impress the mind with the exquisite horror of their reality" (146). Words cannot represent the world's "exquisite horror," since words denote presence and are functionally incapable of communicating the annihilation of meaning. When Augustus's diseased body falls apart at Arthur's incautious touch, "the sea in all directions around was much agitated, and full of strong whirlpools" (157). It is a sea, for Poe, much like the world of men, filled with inarticulate foam and frenzy. Like Caleb Williams, Arthur gazes into the hearts of other men to discover himself; but the person he discovers is not the sort of person anyone in their right mind would care to meet.

Arthur learns to distrust the company of his fellow men, so when he glimpses the ship that will finally (and only temporarily) rescue him, he grows more suspicious than hopeful. At the *Jane Guy*'s approach, he feels "alarmed" to notice its "full crew" gazing out at him, since real men now seem to him as terrible as corpses. As he explains: "'We could hardly imagine it possible that she did not observe us, and were apprehensive that she meant to leave us to perish as we were—an act of fiendish barbarity, which, however incredible it may appear, has been repeatedly perpetrated at sea, under circumstances very nearly similar, and by beings who were regarded as belonging to the human species'" (160).

Pym fears the *Jane Guy*'s approach because, as he explains in a footnote, ships' crews often discover shipwrecked sailors only to abandon them again "to the inexpressible disappointment of the starving and freezing men" (160). As a *Bildungsroman*, Pym's object lesson aboard the *Grampus* is that he should distrust any appearance of salvation—especially when it comes disguised as other men.

The Wreck of the Jane Guy: Mobs, Blacks, and Atrocity in Southern Reactionary Thought

Lowell is a ranting abolitionist and deserves a good using up. It is a pity that he is a poet.

—Edgar Allan Poe, letter to Frederick W. Thomas[18]

I really perceive that vanity about which most men merely prate—the vanity of the human or temporal life. I live continually in a reverie of the future. I have no faith in human perfectibility. I think that human exertion will have no appreciable effect upon humanity. Man is now only more active—not more happy—nor more wise, than he was 6000 years ago. The result will never vary—and to suppose that it will, is to suppose that the foregone man has lived in

*vain—that the foregone time is but the rudiment of the
future—that the myriads who have perished have not been
upon equal footing with ourselves—nor are we with our
posterity. I cannot agree to lose sight of man the individual,
in man the mass.*

—Edgar Allan Poe, letter to James R. Lowell[19]

Arthur, like Caleb, characterizes himself as a scientist, a pur-
veyor of raw data, particularly during his early journal entries
describing his escape from the psychological wreck of the *Grampus* or in his later entries recording nautical discoveries aboard
the *Jane Guy*. Though Arthur persuades the *Jane Guy*'s captain to
pursue his journey into the world's heart, he never regrets the
consequences of his actions—even when they result in the whole-
sale slaughter of the captain and his crew. Instead, he believes he
"must still be allowed to feel some degree of gratification at having been instrumental, however remotely, in opening to the eye
of science one of the most intensely exciting secrets which has
ever engrossed its attention" (187).

Arthur's professed "style" of gathering "minute and connected"
facts proves more appropriate to relating details about the *Jane
Guy*'s fact-finding journey than it does to describing mutiny and
cannibalism aboard the *Grampus*. The inability of words to express the world's "exquisite horror" does not diminish Arthur's
exposition of sea currents, trade routes, and foreign cultures.
Arthur slips so readily into the expositional mode, in fact, that it
seems to act as a sort of panacea, a means of repressing the
world's violence beneath layers of hard detail. Such objective, un-
emotional information pretends to attach firm meaning to an unstable world while denying its basic, inexpressible violence. The
moment Arthur begins keeping his log of the *Jane Guy*'s polar
expedition, he ceases to reflect upon the horrors of his earlier
adventures. By traveling across the ocean's wide spaces, he seems
to believe he has escaped the nightmare of his own disintegrat-
ing body.

Despite Arthur's attempts to make the world seem rational and
scientific, its irrational violence emerges anyway in the form of
what Arthur describes as "primitive black savages." The blacks in
Too-Wit's village possess no real language, only crazed "jabber-
ing" (190). One of their few distinct words, "Tekeli-li," acts as a

primal enunciation of racial alterity. For Poe, black and white are not merely categories of race but of consciousness, biology, and chemistry. Each race possesses a chemical integrity which does not allow mixing. Industriously scribbling his notes, Arthur searches the natural world for scientific explanations and discovers an apartheid of cultural physics. After "collecting a basinful" of water

> and allowing it to settle thoroughly, we perceived that the whole mass of liquid was made up of a number of distinct veins, each of a distinct hue; that these veins did not commingle; and that their cohesion was perfect in regard to their own particles among themselves, and imperfect in regard to neighboring veins . . . The phenomena of this water formed the first definite link in that vast chain of apparent miracles with which I was destined to be at length circled. (194)

This "insoluble" identity of black and white represents one of the world's fundamental "miracles" for Poe and his fellow antiabolitionists; as the advocates of slavery agree again and again, blacks and whites are created fundamentally unequal simply because, as Poe himself explains, it has been since the beginning of time "the will of God it should be so." As a fellow proslavery ideologue, Josiah C. Nott, explains in his "The Natural History of the Caucasian and Negro Races," "there is a Genus, Man, comprising two or more species—that physical causes cannot change a white man into a negro, and that to say this change has been effected by a direct act of providence, is an assumption which cannot be proven, and is contrary to the great chain of Natures Laws."[20] The fundamental law of nature does not decree that all people should live together, but apart. Human nature is implicit with fragmentation, discord, mutiny, and genetic conflict.

According to Poe, blacks should not be suppressed because they are weak but because they are as wildly powerful as the storms that destroy ships or the revolutions that destroy nations. Because blacks are powerful, they must be controlled; the Nat Turner rebellion was not used by slavery's proponents to prove how unhappy slaves were but to justify keeping their irrationality bound up in chains.[21] The monochromatic villages Pym encounters contain black men, women, sheep, cows, flowers, icons, and plants. As Pym describes them: "The dwellings were of the most miserable description imaginable, and, unlike those of even the lowest of the savage races with which mankind are acquainted, were of no uniform plan" (195). The blacks arrive into the white world from outside human history; they don't descend from common early ancestors. They belong to an alien way of being that lacks any kind of "uniform plan," unless, of course, it is for the destruction of all plans.

Everything about Too-Wit's village conceals a threat, even the "obliging" women whose "apparent kindness of disposition was only the result of a deeply laid plan for our destruction" (205). Pym's psychological lessons aboard the *Grampus* have prepared him now for even more brutal instructions. The existence of "natural man" implies not only rebellion against a political system but the total annihilation of everybody in it, just as mutiny aboard the *Grampus* ultimately leads to men devouring one another.

When Arthur first hears the explosion that destroys the *Jane Guy's* crew, he describes it as "a concussion resembling nothing I had ever before experienced, and which impressed me with a vague conception, if indeed I then thought of anything, that the whole foundations of the solid globe were suddenly rent asunder, and that the day of universal dissolution was at hand" (207). Violence washes over the whites like a wave, and everyone is "borne down at once, overwhelmed, trodden under foot, and absolutely torn to pieces in an instant" (215). For Poe, the revolution of blacks totally destroys human life and civil order. It is the cultural and geographic extension of humanity's irrepressible perversity. What people can do to one another they can also do to entire nations. If even civilized individuals such as Pym conceal the savage nature of Peters (that creature who fulfills Pym's unvocalized hatred of Parker by peremptorily slaughtering him), then white society can just as easily conceal the natural forces of its own destruction. For Poe, blacks are the living embodiment of white unreason.

Poe's stories are always about power; and the man who wields the most power in any Poe work is always Poe himself.[22] As prime mover, Poe controls the very text into which his powerless subsidiary author, Pym, is always vanishing. Pym is incapable of writing well or reading accurately; he can decipher neither the message carried to him by his dog, Tiger, nor the intentions of the black races of Tsalal, nor the runes carved in the floors of a cave. As John Carlos Rowe observes, once Arthur boards the *Grampi* he enters "a space that is implicitly textual," and even when Arthur extends his journeying beyond the *Grampus* he encounters a world pervaded by that abstract whiteness which binds and contextualizes black figures in a book.[23] Whiteness describes the world of pure poetic language which Pym can only guess at and which Poe himself inhabits like a righteous God. It is a language divorced from the ugly rude brutality of nature and human utterance, where great artists can divorce themselves from cannibalism, blacks, and democratically stupid readers. Like Pym misinterpreting the hieroglyphs of the cave, common people cannot even read what Harry Levin has called "the scriptural handwriting on the wall": the hand of a black man upraised against the South.[24] Dazzled by the whiteness of pages without words, adrift in a world of white birds, white ash, and white men, common men like Pym cannot even glimpse the poet behind the writing.[25]

In the same way that the black letters which spell Pym's name vanish into the whiteness of Poe's novel, the blacks of Tsalal vanish into the whiteness of another race. "And now we rushed into the embraces of the cataract," Pym recalls in his diary, just before he and the diary are swallowed up by white water. "But there arose in our pathway a shrouded human figure, very far larger in its proportions than any dweller among men. And the hue of the skin of the figure was the perfect whiteness of the snow" (239). The power of blackness may trigger explosions and incite mutinies, but the flash of annihilation that results is supremely and enduringly white.

Sublimating Revolution in "The Fall of the House of Usher"

We may observe here that profound *ignorance on any particular topic is always sure to manifest itself by some allusion to "common sense" as an all-sufficient instructor.*

—Edgar Allan Poe, reviewing the work of James Russell Lowell[26]

Poe does not believe in human progress, much less in human perfectibility. In his sympathetic review of a proslavery tract, Poe suggests that Man's belief in self-improvement overlooks his in-

tractably vulgar nature, for no matter how far science or the arts
may appear to improve and develop, Man himself, "in all his mu-
tations, never fails to get back to some point at which he has been
before. The human mind seems to perform, by some invariable
laws, a sort of cycle, like those of the heavenly bodies."[27] If Poe
envisions cosmology as a recurring cycle, where men appear to
progress only by falling into a process of infinite regression, then
presumably even class revolution returns Mankind to its original
state of savagery; history does not take men into new worlds they
have never known before, but back into old worlds they have
been trying to forget. In Poe's reactionary universe, revolution is
implicit with its own disavowal.

Poe's essay goes on to describe a series of complementary natural relationships: the growth of human knowledge, the catastrophic cycles of planets, "the orbit of the human mind," and the
subversion of private property (267). The revolutions of people
and planets never establish better governments and stabler solar
systems but rather return them to the primordial soup. And no
matter how "eccentric" the orbits of human revolutions, Poe
continues, "what especially concerns us, is to mark its progress
through our planetary system, to determine whether in coming
or returning it may infringe upon us, and prove the messenger of
that dispensation which, in the end of all things, is to wrap our
earth in flames" (267).

Poe's apocalyptic cosmology reduces all political or worldly existence to the "dispensation" of "flames," reestablishing an indisputable authority of pure intellect. As Poe succinctly explains in
Eureka, every universal "deviation from normality involves a
tendency to return to it."[28] Poe's cosmology presumes that transgression ultimately leads us back to a long fallen primal Unity,
but only by destroying us first. By invoking worldly annihilation,
transgression recalls vanquished aristocrats by destroying that vulgar democracy of transitory beings that originally deposed them.

According to Poe's version of both cosmic and American history, democratic revolution subverts the universe with "fanati-
cism and irreligion" (267), since human minds are constantly
"rushing" between these two "extremes." "Under such excitement," Poe explains, "the many who want, band themselves together against the few who possess; and the lawless appetite of
the multitude for the property of others calls itself the spirit of
liberty" (267–268). Recalling the crazed blacks of Pym's polar ex-

pedition, these delirious exponents of liberty never establish superior institutions so much as destroy anything and everything that gets in their way; Poe detects in this "spirit of liberty" a chaotic force which destroys the "governmental machinery" of nations by asserting that "all things be in common!" (268). Like the Masque of the Red Death, democratic revolution reduces bodies and governments to carnival and hysteria. As Poe explains:

> In the history of the French Revolution, we find a sort of symptomatic phenomenon, the memory of which was soon lost in the fearful exacerbation of the disease. But it should be remembered now, that in that war against property, the first object of attack was property in slaves; that in that war on behalf of the alleged right of man to be discharged from all control of law, the first triumph achieved was in the emancipation of slaves. (269)

Here the predication of Poe's apocalyptic cosmology becomes clearer. Just as the mutineers of *Pym* are engulfed by a far more elemental violence than their own (that threat of the black man universalized as the power of blackness itself), Poe sees in revolution that moment of transgression which confuses the identities of black slave and white master, a primal dislocation which leads to vaster political dislocations of property, authority, hegemony, and law. As Poe continues:

> The recent events in the West Indies, and the parallel movement here, give an awful importance to these thoughts in our minds. They superinduce a something like despair of success in any attempt that may be made to resist the attack on all our rights, of which that of Domestic Slavery (the basis of all our institutions) is but the precursor. It is a sort of boding that may belong to the family of superstitions. All vague and undefined fears, from causes the nature of which we know not, the operations of which we cannot say, are of that character. Such apprehensions are alarming in proportion to our estimate of the value of the interest endangered; and are excited by every thing which enhances that estimate. (269)

Poe interprets a widespread political reality—the disintegration of slave institutions in both America and the West Indies—as a sign of metaphysical distress. The "attack" on the "rights" of men to own slaves generates "a sort of boding" about the very nature of

existence. The subversion of political institutions excites "vague
and undefined fears," that inspecific dread which Poe describes again and again in his stories and letters. Poe sublimates fears about class revolt into a scheme of uneasy subjectivity; the "causes of nature" create a sense of disorder which transcends nature as metaphysic and infuses the individual as neurosis. The unstable self, adrift in an unstable world, tries to escape into a wider, re-demptive universe of imagination and art where the horrors of living are constrained by literary form and human intelligence. For Poe, art is the ultimate power trip. It not only transcends the world but envelops and controls it.

Poe dreaded slaves for the same reason he dreaded democrats—they trusted too much in the world's sensuality. Like the most literal-minded misreaders of *Pym*, common citizens were easily duped by hoaxes, since they believed facts spoke for themselves and were not involved in a secret conspiracy of artistic intention. As Harry Levin writes, "In the troubled depths of Poe's uncon-scious, there must have been not only the fantasy of a lost heri-tage, but a resentment and a racial phobia."[29] Poe despised blacks and democratic mobs because they reminded him of the flesh he could live without and the class superiority he wanted to regain.

While many critics have noted that Usher's house represents a sort of mind (one belonging to Usher, Poe, or even abstract Thought itself), the house as it is first described in the story rep-resents both aristocratic order and hereditary estate. As the nameless narrator explains, both Usher's nervous malady and the house's crumbling sentience are implicit with "a constitutional and a family evil" (66). Reflecting upon Roderick's "excessive and habitual" isolation, the narrator explains Roderick's weird behav-ior as a manifestation of the Usher family's congenitally "artistic" intellect and concludes that his current malaise is not psycho-logical so much as genealogical. As the narrator goes on to explain:

> I was aware . . . that his very ancient family had been noted,
> time out of mind, for a peculiar sensibility of temperament,
> displaying itself, through long ages, in many works of exalted
> art, and manifested, of late, in repeated deeds of munificent
> yet unobtrusive charity, as well as in a passionate devotion to
> the intricacies, perhaps even more than to the orthodox and
> easily recognisable beauties, of musical science. (63)

Like Godwin's Falkland, the Usher family is noted for its reserve, its charity, and its "peculiar temperament"; its members prefer to abstractly gaze at stars rather than soberly examine the mundane world. They habitually create enduring monuments of timeless and "exalted art," operate socially as "unobtrusive" agents, and are characterized by their concern with the not "easily recogniz-able" aspects of "musical science." Their finest attributes are privileged, unusual, and secret; in order to maintain their status as poets and artists, they must distance themselves from the unenlightened masses. As the narrator quickly points out, the strange "glow" and "ghastly pallor" of Roderick's expression lacks "any idea of simple humanity" (65). Roderick's character, like that of his entire family, is something more than human and just slightly less than divine.

By virtue of their aesthetic "temperament," the Ushers recog-nize a better and more permanent world than the one their house is built on; their family estate extends beyond the world and into the ether. But while the Usher temperament exists "time out of mind," the narrator and local peasantry impudently express more trivial attentions: they are not concerned with the rarefied do-mains of Usher's art, sensibility, and intellect but rather with the material attributes of his estate, genealogy, and financial worth. Like the nameless narrator, Usher's neighbors prefer to evaluate the House's material dimensions rather than contemplate the fa-mily's intellectual integrity. After noting the apparently "eternal" character of the Usher "malady," the narrator goes on to describe how Usher's house is perceived by the neighboring "peasantry":

> I had learned, too, the very remarkable fact, that the stem of
> the Usher race, all time-honoured as it was, had put forth, at
> no period, any enduring branch; in other words, that the en-
> tire family lay in the direct line of descent, and had always,
> with very trifling and very temporary variation, so lain. It
> was this deficiency, I considered, while running over in
> thought the perfect keeping of the character of the premises
> with the accredited character of the people, and while specu-
> lating upon the possible influence which the one, in the long
> lapse of centuries, might have exercised upon the other—it
> was this deficiency, perhaps, of collateral issue, and the conse-
> quent undeviating transmission, from sire to son, of the patri-
> mony with the name, which had, at length, so identified the
> two as to merge the original title of the estate in the quaint

and equivocal appellation of the "House of Usher"—an appel- lation which seemed to include, in the minds of the peasantry who used it, both the family and the family mansion. (63)

Like proficient Caleb or ludicrous Pym, the narrator submits the empirical world to his personal judgment. After noting that the Ushers possess a "peculiar" and timeless character, one which both preexists and outlasts the world, the narrator goes on to contradict his own observation by deciding that the estate's condition has influenced the character of its inhabitants; the family, in other words, is the product of its environment. Like the peasants who believe the value of the Usher estate determines the family's ultimate "meaning," the narrator believes that property gives people identity, and not vice versa; he belongs to a class that pays more attention to the material than the spiritual. Considering Roderick's mind impenetrable, the narrator rarely looks beyond Roderick's house and physical condition in order to understand his mental disease or his family's timeless "malady."

Time and again, the narrator proves to be a competent witness of events and a lousy analyst of the human soul. The overly empirical narrator describes the facelike house but without recognizing the face of Roderick in it. He moves through the house cataloging items, rooms, and bookshelves but never locates the source of Usher's melancholy. He seeks to solve the "mystery" of the estate's terrible blackness, but its solution lies entirely beyond his reach; Roderick alone perceives the spiritual malaise that consumes him, gazing out from his castle mournfully at the metaphysical harmonies of another world while dreading the material degradations of this one.

Usher's estate fills the narrator with that dread common "to the after-dream of the reveller upon opium—the bitter lapse into everyday life—the hideous dropping off of the veil" (62). The world of property pulls people down into the fatal earth, turning them into lists of dead possessions—walls, trees, windows, sedges, and doors. While traveling across the Usher estate, the narrator feels "an unredeemed dreariness of thought which no goading of the imagination could torture into aught of the sublime" (62). The narrator's limited and literal imagination only perceives nature and property, never penetrating through to deeper truths. He wants the dream of the opium eater, but all he ever gets is blunt reality. Contemplating his nameless dread of the house, the narrator decides:

It was a mystery all insoluble; nor could I grapple with the shadowy fancies that crowded upon me as I pondered. I was forced to fall back upon the unsatisfactory conclusion, that while, beyond doubt, there *are* combinations of very simple natural objects which have the power of thus affecting us, still the analysis of this power lies among considerations beyond our depth. It was possible, I reflected, that a mere different arrangement of the particulars of the scene, of the details of the picture, would be sufficient to modify, or perhaps to annihilate its capacity for sorrowful impression; and, acting upon this idea, I reined my horse to the precipitous brink of a black and lurid tarn that lay in unruffled lustre by the dwelling, and gazed down—but with a shudder even more thrilling than before—upon the remodelled and inverted images of the gray sedge, and the ghastly tree-stems, and the vacant and eye-like windows. (62–63)

Every time the narrator seems on the verge of recognizing a reality greater than the material, he fails. At first he suggests that Usher's temperament may be determined by "considerations beyond our depth," but then he goes on to blame it on heredity and estate. After admitting that his own feelings of dread are incomprehensible, he explains them as possible effects of the very material house of Usher. Believing that a "different arrangement" of sensations will affect him in a more pleasing manner, he steps to the "precipitous brink" of the tarn, where he discovers the house's "inverted" and "lustrous" reflections. Like a great poem or painting, the tarn doesn't simply reflect the world but rearranges it into a more pleasing composition. The narrator quickly realizes that the tarn, like Roderick's feverish imagination, possesses the "capacity" to "annihilate" "sorrowful impression," to annihilate, in fact, the environmental conditions of the mind that observes it.

Yet even when the narrator stumbles upon the imaginative intelligence of the Usher house, he misunderstands its significance. As he continues:

I had so worked upon my imagination as really to believe that about the whole mansion and domain there hung an atmosphere peculiar to themselves and their immediate vicinity—an atmosphere which had no affinity with the air of heaven, but which had reeked up from the decayed trees, and the gray wall, and the silent tarn—a pestilent and mystic vapour, dull,

sluggish, faintly discernible, and leaden-hued. Shaking off
from my spirit what *must* have been a dream, I scanned more
narrowly the real aspect of the building. (64)

The narrator notes the tarn's "mystic vapour"—what Usher himself identifies as the house's imaginative consciousness—only to
dismiss its effects, shaking them off as if they are the products of
a frivolous "dream," preferring to examine the house's "real" fea-
tures rather than its awful radiance; he even has the audacity to
define his lack of any deep philosophical insight as the penetration of a "scrutinising observer" (64).

Though the narrator describes his friend's physical characteris-
tics in great detail, Roderick's actual "manner" strikes him "with
an incoherence—an inconsistency" (65). Just as the nameless
narrator of Poe's detective stories must have everything explained
to him by Dupin, the nameless narrator of "Usher" lacks enough
imagination to explain the world to himself. The narrator is not
Poe's ideal artist, someone capable, as Vincent Buranelli explains,
of being "an interpreter who adapts his experience to the needs
of his imaginative vision and creates his own private universe
from the wreckage he has made of the 'real' world."[30] Roderick,
on the other hand, wants to transform the "wreckage" of his estate into works of art; he composes "wild improvisations" on his
"speaking guitar" and paints fantastic landscapes. Meanwhile,
the baffled narrator proves incapable of "describing" the exact
character of these works. Even while he relentlessly describes furniture, scenery, and buildings, the narrator never makes sense of
art or understands its power to dissociate mind from world.

Like the tarn's "mystic vapour," Roderick's "excited and highly
distempered ideality threw a sulphurous lustre over all" (68).
Thrilled by his friend's fabrications, the narrator identifies the im-
penetrability of Roderick's songs and paintings as the hallmark of
Roderick's genius. As he explains:

From the paintings over which his elaborate fancy brooded,
and which grew, touch by touch, into vaguenesses at which I
shuddered the more thrillingly, because I shuddered knowing
not why;—from these paintings (vivid as their images now
are before me) I would in vain endeavor to educe more than a
small portion which should lie within the compass of merely
written words. By the utter simplicity, by the nakedness of his
designs, he arrested and overawed attention. (68)

Like that buried truth which Caleb's gaze discloses, Roderick's visions "arrest" their perceiver, making the narrator powerless and "overawed." The narrator cannot comprehend but only adore the "nakedness" and "simplicity" of Roderick's paintings; unlike Caleb, Poe's narrator penetrates the aristocrat to discover his inability to understand him. He feels at once baffled and submissive, "overawed" and "arrested" by a world he cannot describe within "the compass of merely written words."

One of Roderick's most "phantasmagoric conceptions" describes his family's intellect and his house's architecture as completely impenetrable:

> A small picture presented the interior of an immensely long and rectangular vault or tunnel, with low walls, smooth, white, and without interruption or device. Certain accessory points of the design served well to convey the idea that this excavation lay at an exceeding depth below the surface of the earth. No outlet was observed in any portion of its vast extent, and no torch, or other artificial source of light was discernible; yet a flood of intense rays rolled throughout, and bathed the whole in a ghastly and inappropriate splendour. (68)

In Roderick's dream of the deep earth, consciousness replaces illumination, not in order to reveal its surroundings but to advertise its own interior "splendour." Unlike the narrator, whose descriptions reflect the dull light of things that exist, Roderick's diseased imagination casts a weird feverish glow, generating original fancies and conceptions. While the narrator characterizes his own eye as "scrutinising," he characterizes Roderick's eye (just as Roderick describes the "windows" of the Haunted Palace) as "luminous" (65, 69). Roderick does not look into the world but projects his own light. Unlike Pym or the narrator, he does not relate facts and events but creates visions.

Works of art, Poe contends, transcend "passion, or even truth" because "true artists will always contrive, first, to tone them into subservience to the predominant aim, and, secondly, to enveil them, as far as possible, in that Beauty which is the atmosphere and the essence of the poem."[31] Artists do not represent the world; they control it. Roderick entombs Madeline because he wants to repress the body, both hers and his own; by repressing the body, Roderick hopes to keep his mind (and the mind of his family) clean, supreme, and uncontestable. The body reminds the aristo-

crat of the worldly authority he cannot maintain and his primal
intelligence which will prevail long after his body has been con-
sumed by worms. To this extent, the body's burial both represses
and sublimates. According to the narrator, Roderick decides to
place Madeline's apparently lifeless body in a vault which is

> small, damp, and entirely without means of admission for
> light; lying, at great depth, immediately beneath that portion
> of the building in which was my own sleeping apartment. It
> had been used, apparently, in remote feudal times, for the
> worst purposes of a donjon-keep, and, in later days, as a place
> of deposit for powder, or some other highly combustible sub-
> stance, as a portion of its floor, and the whole interior of a
> long archway through which we reached it, were carefully
> sheathed with copper. The door, of massive iron, had been,
> also, similarly protected. Its immense weight caused an un-
> usually sharp grating sound, as it moved upon its hinges.
> (71–72)

Roderick wants to conceal within the "donjon-keep" evidence of
nature's revolutionary victory over bodies. Like revolution itself,
democratic nature (the corruption of bodies which makes everybody equal) is as "combustible" as gunpowder. Madeline's body
becomes a prisoner of "remote feudal times," preserved behind
massive walls while remaining detectible to anybody who possesses Roderick's genteel senses. The body of the aristocrat must
be dominated as completely as the bodies of slaves; and the attempt to restrain flesh behind "massive" doors incites a return of
the repressed which destroys man, house, and family estate, re-
ducing everything to the tarn's primordial muck and the imagination's delusory radiance. The reign of nature is as brief as the
flash of annihilation; the reign of Thought (that "Original Unity"
of *Eureka* which is always in the process of being regained) lasts
forever.

The unimaginative narrator, by subordinating emotions to
facts and mind to world, never comprehends what Roderick tries
to teach him. Roderick recites "The Haunted Palace" in order to
illustrate his theory about "the sentience of all vegetable things"
(70), arguing that the world does not shape the mind but rather
that mind *is* world and indivisible from it. As the narrator in-
credulously recounts, Usher considers his family mansion and private intellect to be co-extensive:

The conditions of the sentience had been here, he imagined, fulfilled in the method of collocation of these stones—in the order of their arrangement, as well as in that of the many *fungi* which overspread them, and of the decayed trees which stood around—above all, in the long undisturbed endurance of this arrangement, and in its reduplication in the still waters of the tarn. Its evidence—the evidence of the sentience—as to be seen, he said . . . in the gradual yet certain condensation of an atmosphere of their own about the water and the walls. The result was discoverable, he added, in that silent, yet importunate and terrible influence which for centuries had moulded the destinies of his family, and which made *him* what I now saw him—what he was. Such opinions need no comment, and I will make none. (70)

The narrator cannot believe Roderick's wild suppositions because they directly contradict his own. Suffering under a sort of "democratic fallacy," the narrator, like Godwin and Rousseau, believes nature has shaped the Ushers into what they appear to be. Usher's speculation about a guiding, organized intelligence investing both property and art seems utterly ludicrous to him. For the narrator, spirit is something divorced from the empirical world and responsible to it; physical sensations effect spiritual and mental states. But for Usher, as for Poe, spirit and matter are composed of the same universal substance. World doesn't effect mind, and mind doesn't effect world; instead, both are embraced and invested by the same universe, a single unified field of force and mind. A bad narrator sees significance in the fragmentary: individuals, houses, furniture, events. A brilliant narrator lends meaning to the fragmentary world by imposing form and conveying the big picture.

Poe's nostalgic monarchy of pure thought inverts the normal democratic assumptions of revolution, though at first glance the structural oppositions may seem familiar:

Nature/Intellect
Body/Mind
Madeline/Roderick
Narrator/The House of Usher

For the narrator, domination reads from left to right. He believes that nature conditions intellect, bloody Madeline destroys blood-

less Roderick, dying bodies infect living minds, and he as observer
can correctly ascertain how material conditions affect both his and Roderick's imaginative lives. What the narrator actually discovers, however, is not Godwin's immutable truth but only his own inability to recognize truth when he sees it; and, unlike Poe, the narrator is a lousy critic. When hearing Roderick's "dirges" or observing his paintings, the narrator recalls that after being exposed to these "vaguenesses" he always "shuddered the more thrillingly, because I shuddered knowing not why" (68). The narrator lacks the ability to analyze art, so he can only submit to its power.

By disregarding the true significance of "The Haunted Palace" (he interprets it as Roderick's recognition that his diseased mind has been "trespassed" by the material "kingdom of inorganization"), the narrator overlooks the possibility that any rational intelligence may be at work in the world. Just because the house collapses, the mind behind it doesn't necessarily collapse with it.[32] While houses disintegrate into fragments, the life of the mind finds its way back to wholeness and meaning, the same kind of formal clarity that embraces a good poem or a perfect short story.

Roderick's melancholia marks him as a mind too sensitive for nature; like the princess discomfited by a pea, his sensibilities extend deeper into the world than those of normal men. With his "morbid" sensitivity, he senses his own flesh decaying, his sanity unraveling, and the sounds of his sister clawing a way out of her premature crypt. While Roderick detects Madeline's movements underneath his House, the vulgar narrator detects nothing but his own anxiety.

Madeline's reemergence from the tomb occurs both underneath the narrator's feet and beyond his comprehension. No matter how much noise Madeline makes, the narrator hears nothing but his own bewilderment. Though he feels supernaturally "infected" by Roderick's profound melancholia, he blames his "nervousness" on the "bewildering influence of the gloomy furniture of the room— of the dark and tattered draperies, which, tortured into motion by the breath of a rising tempest, swayed fitfully to and fro upon the walls, and rustled uneasily about the decorations of the bed" (72–73). The narrator's attempt to explain away all psychic phenomena as rational or empirical effects of the world proves "fruitless," and his search for an explanation leads him to gaze into the wide inarticulate spaces of the unknowable. Compelled by some "instinctive spirit," the narrator begins to detect in the "intense darkness" of his own room "certain low and indefinite sounds which came, through the pauses of the storm, at long intervals, I know not whence" (72–73).

The "indefinite" quality of the sounds arouses the narrator's most "intense sentiment of horror," drawing him into a world of chaos where democratic reason fails to operate. Unlike Poe's fallen aristocrats, Usher and Dupin, the narrator never penetrates to the heart of things or comprehends the storm of unreality raging around the world's superficial order. As a result, he never ascertains the power that holds "dominion" over him (72). Overlooking the primary source of his anxiety, the narrator doesn't even notice the fantastic storm engulfing the mansion as he lies in bed, a storm representing both nature's violence and imagination's sublimation of that violence. Roderick enters the narrator's room and asks him if he has seen the storm, and when the narrator admits he has not, Roderick commands, "But, stay! you shall" (73). Turning off his lantern, Roderick unblinds the window to reveal just the sort of storm the narrator would prefer to disregard:

> It was, indeed, a tempestuous yet sternly beautiful night, and one wildly singular in its terror and its beauty. A whirlwind had apparently collected its force in our vicinity; for there were frequent and violent alterations in the direction of the wind; and the exceeding density of the clouds (which hung so low as to press upon the turrets of the house) did not prevent our perceiving the lifelike velocity with which they flew careering from all points against each other, without passing away into the distance. I say that even their exceeding density did not prevent our perceiving this—yet we had no glimpse of the moon or stars—nor was there any flashing forth of the lightning. But the under surfaces of the huge masses of agitated vapour, as well as all terrestrial objects immediately around us, were glowing in the unnatural light of a faintly luminous and distinctly visible gaseous exhalation which hung about and enshrouded the mansion. (73)

While the narrator attributes his anxiety to the "gloomy furniture," Roderick raptly gazes into the same "mystic vapours" which perplexed the narrator during the story's opening scene. The storm generates its own ethereal light without requiring either stars or lanterns. Its "luminous" vapors orbit the "turrets"

of Roderick's house just as the luminous world of Roderick's diseased imagination adorns the family mansion with paintings and
songs; the darkness of the enveloping storm—projected, the narrator suspects, by the tarn's inverted reflections—generates its
own peculiar light just as Roderick's madness generates its own
perverse reason. If aristocracy cannot prevail over matter, it must
elevate itself to the superior realm of imagination. The reactionary mind of the fallen aristocrat, like both the tarn and Roderick's
diseased mind, is one "from which darkness, as if an inherent
positive quality, poured forth upon all objects of the moral and
physical universe, in one unceasing radiation of gloom" (68).

The light Roderick casts from his "luminous" eyes does not reveal things but wraps them in melancholy recollection. If he cannot retain the world, the privileged man will rule the domain of
imagination instead, attaching his signature to a property which
cannot be subverted by crowds of unruly democrats and black
slaves. In the realm of "literature," Poe explains in "The Power of
Words," "as with law or empire—an established name is an estate
in tenure, or a throne in possession."[33] The material house, like
the decayed body of Augustus, collapses into the undifferentiated
world of nature's "tumultuous shouting sound like the voice of a
thousand waters" (77), recalling the frenzied roar of the crowd.
The house of Usher may collapse, but only after attaching the
name of Usher to the more enduring world of art. Even while the
brick and mortar of the Usher house disintegrates, the sublime
status of the Usher House prevails.

Ratiocination and Counterrevolution:
The Oppression of the Sign

*There is a double entendre in the old adage about Truth in a
Well; but, taking the profundity of Truth as at least one of the
meanings—understanding it to be implied that correct ideas
on any topic are to be fished up only from great depths, and
that to have common sense it is necessary to be abysmal—this
being taken as the moral of the adage, I have no objections
on the spot. The profundity of which so much is said, lies
more frequently in the places where we seek Truth than in
those where we find her. Just as the moderately-sized shop-*

Edgar

Allan

Poe

signs are better adapted to their object than those which are Brobdignagian, so, in at least three cases out of seven, is a fact (but especially a reason) overlooked solely on account of being excessively obvious. It is almost impossible, too, to see a thing that lies immediately beneath one's nose.

—Edgar Allan Poe, *Marginalia*

In "Mellonta Tauta," Poe's futuristic explorers of the past travel through the air reading accounts of "the ancient Amriccans" who "*governed themselves!*—did ever anybody hear of such an absurdity?" (662). Aloft in their balloon, Pundit and Pundita receive a batch of newspapers from the "Kanawdians" and read about the discovery of a cornerstone laid in honor of Cornwallis's surrender to Washington. This remote memory of revolutionary America intrigues Pundita, but only so long as it doesn't get too close. As Pundita explains: "The inscription commemorates the surrender of—what?—why, 'of Lord Cornwallis.' The only question is what could the savages wish him surrendered for. But when we remember that these savages were undoubtedly cannibals, we are led to the conclusion that they intended him for sausage" (666). Just then, Pundita's balloon collapses and falls into the sea, but not before Pundita has time to remark that "*the* great men in those days among the Amriccans, were one John, a smith, and one Zacahary, a tailor" (666). In one brief paragraph, Poe articulates his "poetic" conclusions about the vulgar reality of revolution. Like the mutineers of the *Jane Guy*, revolutionaries feast indiscriminately upon captains, kings, and one another. Even the "great men" of revolution are little more than crude, ill-educated tradesmen; they don't apply their names to the world but adopt their menial occupations as names. The world of revolution is a pathetically literal one; Pundita, on the other hand, does not care to explore language's literal properties but only its poetic tropes. Concluding her letter to a nameless correspondent, she claims she doesn't care whether her letter is ever received or not, "as I write altogether for my own amusement" (323). This "amusement" of language allows for poetic distance from the "cannibalism" of a revolutionary world; because his or her labor never produces value or compensation, the poet can never be corrupted. Instead, the poet exists in a world of pure writing, disentangled from the meanness of referentiality, aloft and disencumbered in a glistening balloon.

The poet uses language not to represent the world but to escape
it. Only by repressing the "truth" of cultural conditions can the
poet regain spiritual unity with the regenerative world of imagination. As Poe explains in his review of *Twice-Told Tales*, a "truly
imaginative intellect" doesn't represent truth but sees to it truth
is "restrained, and in some measure repressed, by fastidiousness
of taste, by constitutional melancholy and by indolence."[34] Art
doesn't reveal nature but tames and controls it. In Poe's tales the
dead, buried in graves, continue to struggle, and disembodied
hearts beat irrepressibly beneath floorboards; yet these revolutions
of nature are always circumscribed by the formal structures of
"tales," "poems," discrete and autonomous "works of art." While
nature makes a mockery of human governments, Poe's notion of
art makes a mockery of nature. As Stephen Railton argues, the
ideal "writer Poe describes in his theoretical statements is not
trying to liberate readers but rather to coerce, even to oppress
them."[35]

Poe's protagonists, like de Sade's, suffer from terrible self-
loathing; they loath their bodies, which decay, and their social
privilege, which never lasts. Just as the aristocrat feels threatened
by democracy's idealization of a "common man" hidden within
him like a sort of *agent provocateur*, Poe's protagonists fear being
reduced to the random and indistinguishable. William Wilson
learns that his aristocratic pretensions not only mark him as a
man of refined temperament but as an object of imitation. Democracy is a nightmare to which he doesn't want to awake.

Like Usher, Wilson belongs to an old and distinguished family
which has transformed him into their representative. Wilson describes himself thus:

> I am the descendant of a race whose imaginative and easily
> excitable temperament has at all times rendered them remark-
> able; and, in my earliest infancy, I gave evidence of having
> fully inherited the family character. As I advanced in years it
> was more strongly developed; becoming, for many reasons, a
> cause of serious disquietude to my friends, and of positive in-
> jury to myself. I grew self-willed, addicted to the wildest ca-
> prices, and a prey to the most ungovernable passions. (80)

Wilson's "imaginative" sense of his own superiority places him in
conflict not only with his friends and family but with the flux
and constraint of his own body. He proves not only "ungovern-
able" to his friends but to his own passions. By the mere sound of

his voice he can establish "household law" over family and friends with the most "supreme and unqualified despotism" (83). For Wilson, power is more important than truth or reason; like Poe armed with his hoaxes, Wilson dupes his friends at cards in order to gain mastery over them. Wilson wants nothing less than the unlimited power to achieve whatever he *wills* and not simply to earn what he deserves. Receiving a healthy allowance from his parents, Wilson seeks "to vie in profuseness of expenditure with the haughtiest heirs of the wealthiest earldoms in Great Britain" (89). In every conceivable way, Wilson yearns to distinguish himself from the mob.

Although Wilson's family attempts to shield him behind both literal and figurative walls (the "prison-like rampart" of his home and that "more ponderous gate" of his academy), he soon finds that "the imperiousness of his disposition" over his classmates is threatened by supernaturally democratic influences (81). Whenever Wilson aspires to privileged status, his double miraculously appears to reflect the horrible sameness he shares with other men, reminding him that even though he considers himself a man of "noble descent," his name will always be "one of those everyday appellations which seem, by prescriptive right, to have been, time out of mind, the common property of the mob" (83).

Wilson loathes being duplicated, even at the level of names, or what he calls "my uncourtly patronymic, and its very common, if not plebeian praenomen" (85). He despises his double for exemplifying the "twofold repetition" of his name, a name already resounding with itself—William, son of Will. It is a name which reflects a democratic sameness rather than situates itself in a hierarchy of class differences. Wilson's double threatens to dissolve him into an anarchic boil of common names and mortal passions. And yet at the same time it is a threat which carries a remembrance of original unity, for when Wilson looks at his double he finds "in his accent, his air, and general appearance, a something which first startled, and then deeply interested me, by bringing to mind dim visions of my earliest infancy—wild, confused and thronging memories of a time when memory herself was yet unborn" (86). For Poe, revolution breaks down the unity of bodies and governments by reminding men—but only special, distinctive, incalculably brilliant men—of the greater unity they left behind and will soon achieve again. "The Man of the Crowd," like the Red Death, threatens to level all distinctions by extending "illimitable dominion over all" (119); but once unreason tri-

umphs and the bodies have been destroyed, a space will exist
again in which a vast, reunified intelligence can put all the pieces
back together.

"We have no aristocracy of blood," Poe bemoans in "Philosophy
of Furniture," but rather one "of dollars."[36] In democratic society
people distinguish themselves according to their material "*display*" of wealth and property; in other words, democrats define
themselves according to their property, just as the neighborhood
peasants define Usher's character in terms of his estate. Such presumptions overlook the distinctions of "blood" recognized in "monarchical countries" (462). For Poe, freedom and privilege lie in
the airier region of names and poetry. In Europe, Poe explains:

> the true nobility of blood, confining itself within the strict
> limits of taste, rather avoids than affects that mere costliness
> in which a *parvenu* rivalry may at any time be successfully
> attempted. The people *will* imitate the nobles, and the result
> is a thorough diffusion of proper feeling. But in America, the
> coins current being the sole arms of the aristocracy, their dis-
> play may be said, in general, to be the sole means of aristo-
> cratic distinction; and the populace, looking always upward
> for models, are insensibly led to confound the two entirely
> separate ideas of magnificence and beauty. (462)

Poe links aristocracy with a sort of formal "beauty," one which
the "insensible" mob stupidly confuses with wealth or property.
The mob confuses the true and inherent distinctions between individuals, unable to tell the difference between crude, imitable
things and ideal or "upward" forms. What Poe refers to as an aristocracy of "blood" actually proves to be one in which poetic
language does not represent the world but actually constitutes it.
As Poe explains in "The Power of Words," an individual word
preexists the world as "an impulse on the air."[37] The "blood" of
aristocratic families, like their proper names, acts as that signifier
which, undiluted by democratic imitation, refers back to the fullness of ancestry and ultimately to the fullness of an originary God
who will be regenerated only after the world of democratic imitation has been utterly destroyed.

As the revived Count Allamistakeo explains in "Some Words
with a Mummy," both the blood and the name of patricians operate "figuratively" (485). Like poetic tropes, the names of patrician families were for the Egyptians "the symbols, or *media*,
through which we offered worship to a Creator too august to be

more directly approached" (485). The spiritual power of words preserves that primal integrity of God which cannot be imitated; for the count, language cannot be copied or interpreted but only wrapped up in rags and preserved in vaults. The mummy's patrician society preserves his physical body in order to defend its collective "book" of knowledge from the clumsy misinterpretations of later generations and common citizens.

Like a mummified nobility which perseveres by passing away, books, Poe explains in his essay on "Anastatic Printing," should not be valued for their cost but rather for their "style," since their abstract form embodies more value than their repeatable information. Poe complains that a book's "literary value" is often disregarded in favor of its "physical or mechanical value as the product of physical labor applied to the physical material."[38] Poe believes the "literary" both subordinates and presupposes labor. The literary disciplines the world; the world does not condition the "literary." The world of democracy limits people, just as material production and labor limit "literature." Poe believes that "in depressing the value of the *physique* of a book, the invention will proportionately elevate the value of its *morale*" (159). Whereas for Cooper the democratic subversion of property titles establishes an ultimately truer signification, for Poe words and language preexist the world of property, acting as a force which shapes the world and doesn't simply represent it. Language shouldn't be written; it should be remembered.

Like Pundita in her balloon or Pym in his journals, Auguste Dupin explores a realm of pure textuality. In "The Murders in the Rue Morgue," Dupin is introduced as a "young gentleman" descended from "an illustrious family, but, by a variety of untoward events, had been reduced to such poverty that the energy of his character succumbed beneath it, and he ceased to bestir himself in the world, or to care for the retrieval of his fortunes" (199). Like Usher, Dupin's hereditary "character" lies submerged in awful reality but never stoops to become part of it; instead, he goes into a sort of mourning for the class privileges he has lost, making himself discrete, solitary, and impenetrable. Possessing the name and riddled income of a fallen aristocrat, Dupin lives with his nameless double, the narrator, in a formerly splendid neighborhood, in "a time-eaten and grotesque mansion, long deserted through superstitions into which we did not inquire, and tottering to its fall in a retired and desolate portion of the Faubourg St. Germain" (200).

Dupin possesses the ability to penetrate the hearts and minds of men without getting too close to them. He transgresses other men's privacies by roaming the illustrious domain of his own imagination; he exerts political force by guarding his private darknesses from the world's explicit light, and at one point goes so far as to brag to the narrator "that most men, in respect to himself, wore windows in their bosoms" (201). The more impenetrable Dupin makes himself, the more transparent other men become; Dupin disdains the real world, preferring a realm of pure language where he and the narrator are constantly occupied by "dreams—reading, writing, or conversing" (200). Dupin prefers games, newspapers, and books to actual events and experiences, because experiences impress themselves upon the individual, while Dupin wants to impress himself on the world.

Dupin's "analytical" intellect enjoys frivolous games such as whist, since a "proficiency in whist implies capacity for success in all those more important undertakings where mind struggles with mind" (198). By preferring games to men, written reports to actual events, and language to reality, and by being "fond of enigmas, of conundrums, of hieroglyphics," Dupin never reflects the world so much as obsessively remembers the brilliant dimensions and gleaming, intricate corridors of his own superior intelligence (197). Dupin does not want to read the world in order to know it better; he wants to win games and solve puzzles in order to assert his own superiority. In "The Murders in the Rue Morgue," Dupin and the narrator spend less than one narrative paragraph investigating the scene of the crime and inspecting clues; by the time Dupin arrives at the scene, in fact, he already knows what happened and what he will find. Dupin solves the mystery by reading the newspapers, remotely evaluating the misinterpretations of clumsy middle- and working-class men and women: a laundress, a tobacconist, a gendarme, a silversmith, a banker, a tailor, a clerk, an undertaker, and a confectioner. While reading about the various tradespeople who have identified the murderer's cries as belonging to an Italian, a Russian, a Frenchman, or a Spaniard, Dupin knows that the world's true horror goes beyond the limited knowledge of most people. Out there in the darkness, wild apes roam without motive or reason, murdering indiscriminately, stealing anything that glitters. Like the *Gazette*, a popular newspaper, common citizens cannot solve crimes because they are afraid to journey into the world's "unusual horror" (210). But for Dupin, whose intelligence does extend beyond the world, "unusual" is just the sort of territory he prefers. "In fact," he concludes, "the facility with which I shall arrive, or have arrived, at the solution of this mystery is in the direct ratio of its apparent insolubility in the eyes of the police" (210). Dupin is willing to accept the most outrageous events because he accepts the world's outrageousness; he doesn't try to explain away brutalities and inconsistencies as the weird crimes of foreigners. He recognizes in them the horrible world of nature.

According to Dupin, language doesn't refer forward to worldly things but rather sideways to other words, puzzles, games, problems. Dupin doesn't enjoy games for themselves but rather for the way they exercise and affirm his isolate intelligence; he doesn't seek to solve problems so much as master the other men who get confused by them. Dupin's "proficiency" as a player, the narrator explains, lies in "that perfection in the game which includes a comprehension of *all* the sources whence legitimate advantage may be derived. These are not only manifold but multiform, and lie frequently among recesses of thought altogether inaccessible to the ordinary understanding" (198).

Dupin never glimpses reality so much as generates his own imaginative half-light; he does not master games and puzzles but explores the secret "recesses" of his own "manifold" understanding. He masters the world by not being part of it; he illuminates crimes by maintaining his own privileged darkness. As the narrator explains, Dupin's most important routines are all accomplished in the night:

> It was a freak of fancy in my friend (for what else shall I call it?) to be enamored of the Night for her own sake; and into this *bizarrerie,* as into all his others, I quietly fell; giving myself up to his wild whims with a perfect *abandon.* The sable divinity would not herself dwell with us always; but we could counterfeit her presence. At the first dawn of the morning we closed all the massy shutters of our old building, lighted a couple of tapers which, strongly perfumed, threw out only the ghastliest and feeblest of rays. By the aid of these we then busied our souls in dreams—reading, writing, or conversing, until warned by the clock of the advent of the true Darkness. (200)

Like Roderick Usher, Dupin rules over a kingdom of Darkness
in order to prevent that darkness from ruling him. It is a place impenetrable to Godwinian notions of rationality and common sense. Only in this isolate and purely textual realm does Dupin find true "abandon" and freedom—a freedom he does not enjoy in the world of men, but only in "that infinity of mental excitement which quiet observation can afford" (200). Unlike the bourgeois foil Prefect G——, Dupin does not measure the scenes of crimes with tape measures and microscopes but rather imaginatively assumes the identities of criminals, trying to think the way they think, and without leaving the privacy of his own home or the integrity of his own mind.

As Shoshana Felman has written about a "marginal" comment in a seminar conducted by Lacan, "If 'The Purloined Letter' is specifically the story of 'the poet's superiority in the art of concealment,' then it is not just an allegory of psychoanalysis but also, at the same time, an allegory of poetic writing."[39] Dupin proves himself superior to both the fallen aristocracy and the bourgeois system of "policing" which takes its place, because as a poet he possesses the power to keep things hidden. He proves his superiority over common men by turning their observations into a better story than they can possibly imagine for themselves; he proves his superiority over the king by guarding his own privacies better than the king guards his. As Poe argues in "Eureka," "*no* truths are *self*-evident" (213). Truth is something that must be manufactured by a poet.

Dupin is enlisted into the case of "The Purloined Letter" out of a desire to protect the queen's privacy from a revolt which threatens to open her to public inspection. Lacan's diagram of the tale's "primal scene" and its repetition has been diagrammed by Felman thus:

(not seeing)		(not seeing)	
KING		POLICE	
Scene I		Scene II	
QUEEN	MINISTER	MINISTER	DUPIN
(seeing that	(seeing the	(seeing that	(seeing the
the king does	letter)	the police	letter)
not see)		do not see)	

Each scene describes the transgression of political authority. In the first scene, Minister D—— purloins the letter, transgresses the queen's private life (a life intimately connected with language and writing), and gains "an ascendancy over the illustrious personage whose honor and peace are so jeopardized" (301). Like Caleb, Minister D—— has penetrated the "guilty" secret of government; unlike Caleb, his transgression does not eliminate darkness but redeploys it. The minister maintains his "power" over the queen by concealing her letter in a different place; as Dupin's nameless companion realizes in one of his few correct surmises, it is the "possession, and not any employment of the letter, which bestows the power" (302).[40]

The repetition of this scene describes Poe's vision of revolution's circular momentum; the purloined letter ultimately ends up in the place it originally started from; like Poe's map of cosmic evolution, the letter moves from order to disorder and then back again. When the queen's power is stolen, the police fill the king's position of false authority, while the minister fills the role of a secret, true authority who must be subverted. When a political revolution is reversed by an intellectual one, the police look foolish and presumptuous. Like Arthur Pym and Usher's nameless confidant, Prefect G—— maps surfaces, but by doing so he conceals pertinent truths. Prefect G——'s meticulous attention to surfaces describes the bourgeoisie's notion of authority as what Foucault characterizes as the "eye of power." Foucault describes the shift in the symbolic representations of authority as one in which the king's "body" is displaced by the middle class's multiplicitous "eye," one which Foucault describes as

> that region of irregular bodies, with their details, their multiple movements, their heterogeneous forces, their spatial relations; what are required are mechanisms that analyse distributions, gaps, series, combinations, and which use instruments that render visible, record, differentiate and compare: a physics of a relational and multiple power, which has its maximum intensity not in the person of the king, but in the bodies which can be individualized by these relations.[41]

Prefect G—— acts as a sort of "relational and multiple power," invading the minister's home with fleets of advisors and lieutenants. Yet Prefect G——'s inability to comprehend power in anything but mechanical and superficial terms causes him to make the absurd declaration that "such a thing as a *secret* drawer is impossible" (303). For Poe, however, secrets are not hidden within the world but within the way minds work; the actual *secret* of power is hidden within the minds of privileged men, among the most inaccessible regions of a truly analytical mind. Prefect G—— thinks he can easily transgress any room, or closet, or drawer, even though Dupin tries to warn him that there is "no such thing as overreaching the Minister" (305). One cannot "overreach" opponents of superior intellect as easily as one can burglarize their apartments. Dupin, after all, has "conquered" Minister D—— long before he enters his hotel room, where he goes not to discover the letter so much as take it home. Long before he retrieves the queen's letter, Dupin has already conquered Minister D——, if only within the privacy of his own mind.

A second repetition occurs in what Lacan refers to as the "primal scene" of "The Purloined Letter." Occurring in the story's final pages, it can be diagrammed as follows:

PREFECT G——
(not seeing)

Scene III

NARRATOR   DUPIN
(not seeing)   (seeing)

In his secret study, Dupin proves himself the only man capable of mastering the letter's power, the only one capable of both concealing and revealing its presence. He has not merely counteracted a revolutionary plot; he has, by his solution to the crime, reinscribed power within a private monarchy of pure thought—his own.

As Dupin explains in "The Murders in the Rue Morgue," "Truth is not always in a well. In fact, as regards the more important knowledge, I do believe that she is invariably superficial" (209). While truth is literally strewn across the world's surface, it never surpasses in importance the quality of intellect which analyzes it. Knowledge and truth lie everywhere, like nature; but when truth is perceived and diagrammed by common men such as Prefect G—— or Pym, it does not show them the way out of nature's prison. In order to find a way out, privileged individuals like Dupin use their imaginative faculty to control knowledge and regain that perfectly unified world that existed before democrats took it all apart. Dupin does not only perceive truth; he recontextualizes it, just as by returning the queen's purloined letter he recontextualizes the existing scheme of political power. When the letter is returned, the queen again rules, but only in a story of which Dupin is the author.

Poe's intellectual aristocrats are not concerned with facts but with their own formal resolution of facts. They do not penetrate surfaces but rearrange those surfaces into a more aesthetically "pleasing" composition. The purloined letter's power resides not in its depth—in its ability to refer to some buried referent—but in its deployment across a formal structure of appearances and relationships. Power resides not in what the letter says but in where it is situated. As Poe explains in *Eureka*, the world's ultimate annihilation will recreate a system of poetic form that existed long before the world ever existed. In political terms, people do not generate meaning and order; they are embraced by a power that preceded their birth. As Poe explains:

> In the construction of *plot*, for example, in fictitious literature, we should aim at so arranging the incidents that we shall not be able to determine, of any one of them, whether it depends from any other or upholds it. In this sense, of course, perfection of plot is really, or practically, unattainable—but only because it is a finite intelligence that constructs. The plots of God are perfect. The Universe is a plot of God. (292)

Just as individuals and their relations must be repressed by one indisputable authority—the divine God, King, or Poet—individual plots and stories imply the more "perfect" plot of God, that ultimate resolution of events which, like the resolutions of Poe's own tales, annihilates the entire world of common and unexemplary transgressions. If the king must die, then the world must die with him, destroyed by his own expiring cry for revenge. By dying, the world rejoins that primal unity over which the dead king eternally presides. For Poe, common people transgress nature in order to establish an authority that existed long before they ever got there. And by the time common people get there, they find themselves already gone.

Notes

INTRODUCTION

1. Michel Foucault, *Language, Counter-Memory, Practice: Selected Essays and Interviews*, ed. Donald F. Bouchard, trans. Donald F. Bouchard and Sherry Simon (Ithaca: Cornell University Press, 1977), 35.

2. Foucault worked on the assumption that Western culture generates its own realm of lawlessness as a means of validating its own lawfulness. The application of his work to problems of poetry and canonization has been discussed by Peter Stallybrass and Allon White, *The Politics and Poetics of Transgression* (Ithaca: Cornell University Press, 1986). Also see Dana B. Polan, "Fables of Transgression: The Reading of Politics and the Politics of Reading in Foucauldian Discourse," *Boundary 2* 10, no. 3 (1982): 361–381; and David Miller, "Foucault and the Concept of Transgression," *Origin* 5 (Spring 1985): 77–89.

3. See, of course, R. W. B. Lewis, *The American Adam: Innocence, Tragedy, and Tradition in the Nineteenth Century* (Chicago: University of Chicago Press, 1955), 1–28.

4. Richard Chase, *The American Novel and Its Tradition* (Baltimore: Johns Hopkins University Press, 1980), 13.

5. Michael Davitt Bell, *The Development of American Romance: The Sacrifice of Relation* (Chicago: University of Chicago Press, 1980), 8–9.

6. For one of the more interesting recent versions of this general argument, see William C. Spengemann, *The Adventurous Muse: The Poetics of American Fiction, 1789–1900* (New Haven: Yale University Press, 1977). Spengemann describes "the emergence of the American Romantic Novel" as a "potentially subversive vision of reality" which challenges the conservative European "poetics of domesticity" (3). Like Fiedler, he describes the movement as one which escapes the stable responsibilities of families and governments and journeys into the wider dynamic freedoms of terra incognita and unlimited exploration. American literature, Spengemann contends, teaches Europeans "to see the world through the

eyes of discovery and to comprehend the vast differences between the world that is seen from an unchanging point and the one seen from a point in motion" (2). As I will try to argue in chapter 2, I think this belief in the radical freedom of American literature is the reigning fallacy of contemporary American criticism. What Spengemann calls the "poetics of adventure" is actually informed by the same ideological and class interests as "the poetics of domesticity." Both genres, in fact, are essentially trying to tell the same story.

7. Henry Nash Smith, *Virgin Land: The American West as Symbol and Myth* (New York: Vintage Books, 1950), 16–37.

8. By "elemental narrative unit" I'm referring to what Fredric Jameson has identified as the "ideologeme," which he defines as follows: "An amphibious formation, whose essential structural characteristic may be described as its possibility to manifest itself either as a pseudoidea—a conceptual or belief system . . .—or as a protonarrative, a kind of ultimate class fantasy about the 'collective characters' which are the classes in opposition." See Jameson, *The Political Unconscious: Narrative as a Socially Symbolic Act* (Ithaca: Cornell University Press, 1981), 87. I'm indebted to this book in its entirety.

1. THE WHOLE TRUTH

1. William Godwin, *Enquiry Concerning Political Justice and Its Influence on Modern Morals and Happiness* (London: Penguin Books, 1985), 288–289.

2. The fixed structural relations usually assigned to Falkland and Caleb have, of course, always-already been deconstructed—and pretty effectively, too, I might add, by Jerrold E. Hogle in "The Texture of Self in Godwin's *Things as They Are*," *Boundary 2* 7 (Winter 1979): 261–281. Unlike Hogle, I'm arguing that the binary oppositions in *CW* don't come loose in the tide of language but are actually made indeterminate by class strategies of revolt. For a standard "binary" reading of Falkland and Caleb as villain and hero, respectively, see Rudolf F. Storch, "Metaphors of Private Guilt and Social Rebellion in Godwin's *Caleb Williams*," *ELH* 34, no. 2 (June 1967): 188–207.

3. Harvey Gross, "The Pursuer and the Pursued: A Study of *Caleb Williams*," *Texas Studies in Literature and Language* 1, no. 3 (1959): 401.

4. William Godwin, *Caleb Williams* (Oxford: Oxford University Press, 1986), 4.

5. Ernst Cassirer, *The Philosophy of the Enlightenment*, trans. Fritz
    C. A. Koelln and James P. Pettegrove (Princeton: Princeton Uni-
    versity Press, 1951), 11.

6. P. N. Furbank, "Godwin's Novels," *Essays in Criticism* 5 (1955):
    216.

7. Jeremy Bentham, "Panopticon Papers," in *A Bentham Reader*,
    ed. Mary Peter Mack (New York: Pegasus Books, 1969), 200.

8. In this and the following passages I am indebted to the work of
    Lukács, Adorno, and Horkheimer in their joint critique of bour-
    geois culture's attempt to "universalise rationalism," as Lukács de-
    scribes it in *History and Class Consciousness: Studies in Marxist
    Dialectics*, trans. Rodney Livingstone (Cambridge: MIT Press,
    1971), 116. To put it very reductively, the Frankfurt School Marx-
    ists tend to argue that individuals who use reason to commodify
    and do violence to the world of nature ultimately do the same vio-
    lence to the nature of themselves. As Horkheimer and Adorno ex-
    plain it, humanity's "world domination over nature turns against
    the thinking subject himself . . . What appears to be the triumph
    of subjective rationality, the subjection of all reality to logical for-
    malism, is paid for by the obedient subjection of reason to what
    is directly given." See *Dialectic of Enlightenment*, trans. John
    Cumming (New York: Seabury Press, 1972), 26. Like Adorno and
    Horkheimer, I'm also arguing that the bourgeoisie's attempt to es-
    tablish a machinery of reason results in an imaginary dream of to-
    tal coercion masquerading as total consensus. I'm also indebted to
    Vincent Pecora, who, in his recent book *Self and Form in Modern
    Narrative*, articulated many of the Frankfurt School's arguments so
    concisely that he reminded me how much they shaped my original
    plans for this book. While I totally disagree with him that the fi-
    nal realization of what he calls the "coercive character" of "en-
    lightened thought" manifests itself in modernism (a movement
    which strikes me as more retrospective in character than Pecora
    seems to suspect), I do agree that this "coercive character" objecti-
    fies human personality in many of the same ways it objectifies nar-
    rative form. See Pecora, *Self and Form in Modern Narrative* (Balti-
    more: Johns Hopkins University Press, 1989), 2.

9. Many commentators have taken these indications of Falkland's di-
    vine power to imply that the relationship between Caleb and Falk-
    land "is really a profound symbolic rendering of the relation be-
    tween God and Man," as Walter Allen suggests in *The English
    Novel: A Short Critical History* (New York: E. P. Dutton and Co.,
    1954), 105. B. J. Tysdahl discusses the influence of Calvinism on
    Godwin's novels in *William Godwin as Novelist* (London: Athlone
    Press, Ltd., 1981), 11–23.

10. Storch, "Metaphors of Private Guilt," 191.

11. Godwin's application of the principles of *Political Justice* to *Caleb Williams* is discussed in Kenneth Graham, *The Politics of Narrative: Ideology and Social Change in William Godwin's Caleb Williams* (New York: AMS Press, 1990), particularly 137–170.

12. The courtroom scene has been discussed by Gerard A. Barker, "Justice to Caleb Williams," *Studies in the Novel* 6 (Winter 1974): 377–388.

13. I'm implicitly disagreeing here with James Thompson's argument that the "biographical" story of Caleb is somehow at odds with the "penological" one. For Godwin, the problems of both prisons and coercion are enacted on the psychological level as well as the social one. See Thompson's "Surveillance in William Godwin's *Caleb Williams*," in *Gothic Fictions: Prohibition/Transgression*, ed. Kenneth W. Graham (New York: AMS Press, 1989), 173–198.

14. Rexford Stamper, "*Caleb Williams*: The Bondage of Truth," *Southern Quarterly* 12, no. 1 (October 1973): 44.

15. D. Gilbert Dumas, "Things as They Were: The Original Ending of *Caleb Williams*," *Studies in English Literature* 6, no. 3 (Summer 1966): 590.

16. Mitzi Meyers, "Godwin's Changing Conception of *Caleb Williams*," *Studies in English Literature* 12, no. 4 (Autumn 1972): 597.

17. I'm referring, of course, to Foucault's notion of "the eye of power," which is well discussed in an interview in *Power Knowledge: Selected Interviews and Other Writings 1972–1977*, ed. Colin Gordon, trans. Colin Gordon et al. (New York: Pantheon, 1980), 146–165. Here Foucault explains that Bentham's dream of the Panopticon can be seen as "the illusion of almost all of the eighteenth-century reformers who credited opinion with considerable potential force. Since opinion could only be good, being the immediate consciousness of the whole social body, they thought people would become virtuous by the simple fact of being observed."

2. THE GREAT SEA-CHANGE

1. Tom Paine, "Common Sense," in *Common Sense, The Rights of Man, and Other Essential Writings of Thomas Paine* (New York: New American Library, 1969), 22–23.

2. Robert Lawson-Peebles discusses some of the ways in which revolutionaries like Paine described the colonization of America as an application of political principles in *Landscape and Written Ex-*

pression in *Revolutionary America* (Cambridge: Cambridge University Press, 1988), 44–57.

3. For a discussion of "sympathy" as a controlling force in revolutionary colonial politics, see Gordon S. Wood, *The Radicalism of the American Revolution* (New York: Alfred A. Knopf, 1992), especially 213–225.

4. Eric Foner, *Tom Paine and Revolutionary America* (New York: Oxford University Press, 1976), 124.

5. Ultimately I'm arguing that American revolutionaries "elided" the facts of class for two reasons, one political and the other ideological. Politically, they used geography to justify their revolt against Britain in order to ameliorate colonial class divisions and thus secure aristocratic support for the rebellion. And ideologically, the westward movement actually erased the class distinction from the most intimate psychology of revolt—the desire of individuals to secure property. Since individuals could acquire property without taking it from a class of their own nation, they unconsciously began to forget that that class even existed.

6. Ralph Ketcham, ed., *The Anti-Federalist Papers and the Constitutional Convention Debates* (New York: New American Library, 1986), 343.

7. Charles Brockden Brown, letter to Henrietta G., in David Lee Clark, *Charles Brockden Brown: Pioneer Voice of America* (Durham: Duke University Press, 1952), 71–72, 98–99.

8. R. W. B. Lewis, *The American Adam: Innocence, Tragedy, and Tradition in the Nineteenth Century* (Chicago: University of Chicago Press, 1955), 91.

9. Leslie A. Fiedler, *Love and Death in the American Novel* (New York: Meridian Books, 1960), 147–148.

10. See also Leslie A. Fiedler, *The Return of the Vanishing American* (London: Jonathan Cape, Ltd., 1968). Here Fiedler argues that for American writers geography has always been "mythological" (14). The closest American writers ever get to a novel of class relations is the one of sexual relations, one in which the man usually disappears into the West in order to avoid the more civilized responsibilities. Fiedler eventually goes on to argue that "it is a *Pagan* Paradise Regained that Americans have dreamed in the forests of the New World, a natural Eden lost when Christianity intervened—which means when woman intervened" (117). Again, I tend to agree with Fiedler that the West serves as a sort of mythological diversion for American writers from the more "European" issues of class politics and culture, but unlike him I am arguing that this very diversion is itself class-oriented, or perhaps class-reoriented.

11. Charles Brockden Brown, *Edgar Huntly; or Memoirs of a Sleep-Walker,* ed. Sydney J. Krause and S. W. Reid (Kent and London: Kent State University Press, 1984), 3.

12. See Donald A. Ringe, *American Gothic: Imagination and Reason in Nineteenth-Century Fiction* (Lexington: University Press of Kentucky, 1982), especially 36–57. Ringe describes Brown's development of the European gothic as a sort of amplification of unreason. Where the fiction of the Radcliffe school tended to resolve narrative conflicts by returning its characters to a "rule of reason," in Brown characters tend to get lost in their own convoluted attempts to wield reason. As I hope to show in the following pages, this escalating unreason of the American romance is involved in a powerful act of forgetting or erasing its own footsteps—those rationalizations which it used to justify its ruthless drive westward. As a result, reason, like civilization, is often left far behind.

13. A number of commentators have discussed the influence of *Caleb Williams* on Brown's other novels, especially *Wieland, Arthur Mervyn,* and *Ormond,* but for my money the influence is especially pronounced in *Edgar Huntly*. William L. Hedges has discussed the connection between *Caleb* and *Edgar,* but he identifies Clithero as the "Irish Caleb Williams" in Brown's version of the detective story, while I'm arguing that both Edgar and Clithero share Caleb's narrative position. See Hedges's "Charles Brockden Brown and the Culture of Contradictions," *Early American Literature* 9, no. 2 (Fall 1974): 107–142. See especially pages 130–133.

14. The influence of Godwin's political philosophy as well as the influence of the French and American Enlightenments on Brown's major novels have been notably discussed by Warner Berthoff, "Brockden Brown: The Politics of the Man of Letters," *Serif* 3, no. 4 (December 1966): 3–11; and in Jay Fliegelman's excellent introduction to Brown's *Wieland and Memoirs of Carwin the Biloquist* (New York: Penguin Books, 1991), vii-xliv.

15. Norman S. Grabo, "Introduction" to *Edgar Huntly, Or, Memoirs of a Sleep-Walker* (New York: Penguin Books, 1988), xxi.

16. The "indefiniteness" of Brown's narratives, and their fundamental inability to reach any sort of convincing resolution, has led some commentators to condemn him as a lousy technician (see, for example, Hedges) and others to praise him as an early Symbolist. Some commentators, such as John Cleman in "Ambiguous Evil: A Study of Villains and Heroes in Charles Brockden Brown's Major Novels," *Early American Literature* 10, no. 2 (Fall 1975): 190–219, analyze his "ambiguities" as deliberately designed to add a sort of New Critical poetic complexity to his work. The most interesting

sustained study of Brown to argue that his wild contrivances and
unresolved subplots are deliberately constructed can be found in
Norman S. Grabo's *The Coincidental Art of Charles Brockden
Brown* (Chapel Hill: University of North Carolina Press, 1981).
Grabo claims that most of the places in Brown that have been
cited by critics as signs of "sloppy craftsmanship" were actually
"purposeful and necessary" (xi). On the contrary, I think Brown
was a lousy craftsman, but partially because the narrative model
he inherited from Godwin didn't quite fit his colonial world. I find
him interesting not because he makes novels that are more indefinite than the world but because he suffers under the same sense of
political indefiniteness as the culture in which he was raised, and
because he helps to transform the story of political conflict into a
story of colonial expansion.

17. The double has been frequently discussed as a recurring motif in
Brown's fiction. For discussions of the double in *Edgar Huntly*, I'd
particularly recommend Sydney J. Krause's introduction to the
novel's Kent State edition, pages xiv-xxiii, cited previously, and
Richard Slotkin, *Regeneration through Violence: The Mythology
of the American Frontier, 1600–1860* (Middletown: Wesleyan University Press, 1973), 382–390.

18. The scene in the cave, as well as its complex deployment of the
term "savage," has been discussed by Arthur G. Kimball, "Savages
and Savagism: Brockden Brown's Dramatic Irony," *Studies in Romanticism* 6, no. 4 (Summer 1967): 214–225.

19. Emerson repeatedly glorifies the transformative nature of human
spirit. See, for example, "Self Reliance," where he writes: "Life
only avails, not the having lived. Power ceases in the instant of
repose; it resides in the moment of transition from a past to a new
state, in the shooting of the gulf, in the darting to an aim. This
one fact the world hates, that the soul *becomes*; for that for ever
degrades the past, turns all riches to poverty, all reputation to
shame." Ralph Waldo Emerson, *Essays and Lectures* (New York:
Library of America, 1983), 271–272.

20. Mark R. Patterson, *Authority, Autonomy and Representation in
American Literature, 1776–1865* (Princeton: Princeton University
Press, 1988), 71. Brown's anxiety about establishing a final ground
of authority, or even of authorship, has also been notably discussed by Emory Elliot, *Revolutionary Writers: Literature and Authority in the New Republic 1725–1810* (New York: Oxford University Press, 1986), 3–54 and 218–270.

21. Brown's use of landscape as a psychological space has been discussed by Sydney J. Krause, "*Edgar Huntly* and the American

Nightmare," *Studies in the Novel* 13, no. 3 (Fall 1981): 294–301, and by George Toles, "Charting the Hidden Landscape: *Edgar Huntly*," *Early American Literature* 16, no. 2 (Fall 1981): 133–153.

3. JAMES FENIMORE COOPER

1. James Fenimore Cooper, *The American Democrat*, ed. George Dekker and Larry Johnston (New York: Penguin Books, 1969), p. 174–175.
2. Jacques Derrida, *Of Grammatology*, trans. Gayatri Chakravorty Spivak (Baltimore and London: Johns Hopkins University Press, 1976), 186.
3. James Fenimore Cooper, *The Pioneers, or the Sources of the Susquehanna; A Descriptive Tale* (Albany: State University of New York Press, 1980), 6.
4. Cooper, one of the only early American authors to write about the dynamics of class rather than those of individual character, has always been of particular interest to Marxist critics. See, for example, Georg Lukács, *The Historical Novel*, trans. Hannah and Stanley Mitchell (1962; London: Merlin Press, 1965), 64–65.
5. John F. Lynen discusses the formal presentation of time and history in Cooper's pictorial art in *The Design of the Present: Essays on Time and Form in American Literature* (New Haven: Yale University Press, 1969), 169–204.
6. This passage always reminds me of de Crèvecoeur, whose politics are as anxiously balanced as Cooper's. For example, when de Crèvecoeur's fictional self-recreation, Farmer John, reflects on the radical freedom of men taking their properties willy-nilly from the wilderness, he recognizes that in a revolutionary culture someone else may come along soon who will want to take his property away from him. In order to defend his rights of tenure as being better and more lasting than anybody else's, he hastily imagines his own legal precedent: "Such is our progress," Farmer John notes, discussing how a certain degeneracy of human character helps civilization find its noble way westward, "such is the march of the Europeans toward the interior parts of this continent. In all societies there are off-casts; this impure part serves as our precursors or pioneers; my father himself was one of that class, but he came upon honest principles and was therefore one of the few who held fast; by good conduct and temperance, he transmitted to me his fair inheritance, when not above one in fourteen of his contemporaries had the same good fortune" (see J. Hector St. John de Crève-

coeur, *Letters from an American Farmer and Sketches of Eighteenth-*
Century America, ed. Albert E. Stone [New York: Penguin Books,
1981], 73). De Crèvecoeur himself certainly never inherited his
American farm from his father, from whom he was estranged; yet
in order to distance himself from the "off-casts" that were making
the West safe for the culture which had cast them off, he invents a
father who proved his natural abilities by establishing residency in
the wilderness and at the same time recovering a set of enduringly
"honest principles" according to which everyone should live. As
we shall see in Cooper, many proponents of revolution likewise in-
vented their own genealogy in order to argue a sort of "natural"
legitimacy over property rights. The complicated process of this
genealogical remapping is brilliantly discussed by Eric Sundquist
in *Home as Found: Authority and Genealogy in Nineteenth-
Century American Literature* (Baltimore: Johns Hopkins University Press, 1979). In Cooper's work, as we shall see, home, like the
father, is a place where the new men of authority are always returning in order to justify the places they have already been. I
hope the importance of this "return" to the source will become
clear by the end of this chapter.

7. Stephen Railton discusses the psychological implications of these
    grave sites in *Fenimore Cooper: A Study of His Life and Imagina-
    tion* (Princeton: Princeton University Press, 1978), 147–193.

8. The most well known example of this ideological rumor is re-
    counted and refuted by Dorothy Waples in *The Whig Myth of
    James Fenimore Cooper* (London: Oxford University Press, 1938).
    However, the notion of an ideological rupture between Cooper's
    early and late work has been well argued by Ross J. Pudaloff in
    "The Gaze of Power: Cooper's Revision of the Domestic Novel,
    1835–1850," *Genre* 17, no. 3 (1984): 275–295.

9. James Fenimore Cooper, *New York* (New York: William Farquhar
    Payson, 1930), 48. Cooper goes on in this passage to argue that
    "the great results" which will be generated by the "settlement of
    America" provide evidence that the nation enjoys the good will of
    "Providence," who "may yet guide us in safety through the period
    of delusion, and the reign of political fallacies, which is fast draw-
    ing around us." For Cooper, the "delusions" and "fallacies" that
    result from colonial expansion are a sort of necessary evil, leading
    men into spaces where they can permanently establish forts of
    reason and stability. This passage from *New York* is discussed by
    John P. McWilliams, Jr., *Political Justice in a Republic: James
    Fenimore Cooper's America* (Berkeley: University of California
    Press, 1972), 109.

10. The ways in which Cooper uses landscape in order to secure a sort

of ahistorical landscape is discussed by H. Daniel Peck, *A World by Itself: The Pastoral Moment in Cooper's Fiction* (New Haven: Yale University Press, 1977), 58.

11. Brook Thomas, "*The Pioneers*, or the Sources of American Legal History: A Critical Tale," *American Quarterly* 36 (1984): 86–111. Also see Charles Swann, "Guns Mean Democracy: *The Pioneers* and the Game Laws," in *James Fenimore Cooper: New Critical Essays*, ed. Robert Clark (London: Vision and Barnes & Noble, 1985), 96–119.

12. Jay Fliegelman, *Prodigals and Pilgrims: The American Revolution against Patriarchal Authority, 1750–1800* (Cambridge: Cambridge University Press, 1982).

13. Quoted by Marius Bewley, *The Eccentric Design: Form in the Classic American Novel* (New York: Columbia University Press, 1959), 29–30.

14. Bernard Bailyn, *The Ideological Origins of the American Revolution* (Cambridge: Belknap Press of Harvard University Press, 1967), 31.

15. James Fenimore Cooper, *The Deerslayer, or The First Warpath* (New York: New American Library, 1980), 534.

16. Donald E. Pease, *Visionary Compacts: American Renaissance Writings in Cultural Context* (Madison: University of Wisconsin Press, 1987), 3–48.

17. See, for example, Richard B. Morris's discussion of violent states' rights border disputes which demonstrated the need for a Federalist constitution in *Witnesses at the Creation: Hamilton, Madison, Jay, and the Constitution* (New York: Holt, Rinehart, and Winston, 1985), 169–185.

18. For a discussion of Natty's hut and colonial American notions of ownership, see Richard Godden, "Pioneer Properties, or 'What's in a Hut?'" in *New Critical Essays*, ed. Clark, 121–141.

19. For an explicit discussion of Cooper's legal beliefs in the context of his time, see Charles Hansford Adams, "*The Guardian of the Law*": *Authority and Identity in James Fenimore Cooper* (University Park: Pennsylvania State University Press, 1990), especially his discussion of *The Pioneers*, pages 55–80. Also, for a discussion of the importance of "gentlemen" in the legal life of a society (figures who represent a sort of ideal primogeniture of reason, sensibility, and education), see Catherine H. Zuckert, *Natural Right and the American Imagination: Political Philosophy in Novel Form* (Savage, Md.: Rowman and Littlefield Publishers, 1970), especially 39–45.

20. For the most recent discussion of this "seasonal" structure of *The Pioneers*, see Donald A. Ringe's introduction to *The Pioneers* (New

York: Penguin Books, 1988), especially x–xiii. Ringe discusses the regressive temporal progress of the novel, as well as its contain- ment of democratic destructiveness within a vaster cycle of decay and regeneration.

117
Notes to
Pages 49–63

21. Thomas Philbrick, "Cooper's *The Pioneers*: Origins and Structure," in *James Fenimore Cooper: A Collection of Critical Essays*, ed. Wayne Fields (New Jersey: Prentice-Hall, 1979), 58–79.

22. For an excellent discussion of Cooper's backward progress, espe- cially as a response to the Three Mile Point controversy, see Don- ald E. Pease's introduction to Cooper's *The Deerslayer* (New York: Penguin Books, 1987), vii-xxv.

23. The backward movement of the Leatherstocking Saga has also been interpreted as a retreat into the womb: see Annette Kolodny, *The Lay of the Land: Metaphor as Experience and History in American Life and Letters* (Chapel Hill: University of North Caro- lina Press, 1975), 89–115.

24. John Jay, *The Federalist Papers*, ed. Clinton Rossiter (New York: New American Library, 1961), 38.

25. James Fenimore Cooper, *The Last of the Mohicans: A Narrative of 1757* (Albany: State University of New York Press, 1983), 1.

26. Dennis W. Allen, "'By all the truth of signs': James Fenimore Cooper's *The Last of the Mohicans*," *Studies in American Fiction* 9 (1981): 159–179; Steven Blakemore, "Strange Tongues: Cooper's Fiction of Language in *The Last of the Mohicans*," *Early American Literature* 19 (1984): 21–41.

27. Eric Cheyfitz discusses translation as an act of colonization in his essay "Literally White, Figuratively Red: The Frontier of Transla- tion in *The Pioneers*," in *New Critical Essays*, ed. Clark, 55–95.

28. Blakemore, "Strange Tongues," 29.

29. For a discussion of how violence operates in *Mohicans* at the lev- els of both plot and language, see Thomas Philbrick, "*The Last of the Mohicans* and the Sounds of Discord," *American Literature* 43 (1971): 25–41.

30. Ralph Waldo Emerson, "Nature," in *Essays and Lectures* (New York: Library of America, 1983), 33.

31. Philbrick provides an interesting discussion of this escalating "dis- cord" ("*The Last of the Mohicans*," 33–35).

32. James Fenimore Cooper, *Home as Found* (New York: Capricorn Books, 1961), 23.

33. Michael Paul Rogin, *Fathers and Children: Andrew Jackson and the Subjugation of the American Indian* (New York: Alfred A. Knopf, 1975), 101. Rogin suggests that in nineteenth-century America, any invalidation of systems of property law threatened to invalidate the very "process by which men appropriated nature.

It exposed them to 'the waspish, hysterical mother,' to contamination, invasion, and control. Fears of 'the mother state' had a practical basis in land disputes, but they also suggest that psychological autonomy was insecurely achieved. Property served Americans, in the Puritan phrase, as the 'outward and visible sign of inward and spiritual grace.' Just as in Protestantism, however, so in the development of childhood independence the symbols of power were filled with ambivalence. Ownership partly expressed anger at bad internal objects and the need to control them."

34. James Fenimore Cooper, "American and European Scenery Compared," in *The Home Book of the Picturesque: or, American Scenery, Art, and Literature*, ed. Motley F. Deakin (1852; Gainesville: Scholars' Facsimiles and Reprints, 1967), 69.

4. EDGAR ALLAN POE

1. Edgar Allan Poe, *The Letters of Edgar Allan Poe*, ed. John Ward Ostrom (New York: Gordian Press, 1966), 2: 438.

2. Edgar Allan Poe, *Essays and Reviews*, ed. G. R. Thompson (New York: Library of America, 1984), 260.

3. Poe, "South-Sea Expedition," in ibid., 1231.

4. Edgar Allan Poe, "Ms. Found in a Bottle," in *The Annotated Tales of Edgar Allan Poe*, ed. Stephen Peithman (New York: Avenel Books, 1981), 20. Unless noted otherwise, all other references to Poe's tales will be to this edition and specified by page numbers within the text.

5. Not much has been written on the extreme differences between Godwin and Poe, but the best discussion of the similarities, particularly in the construction of plot, remains Burton R. Pollin, *Discoveries in Poe* (Notre Dame: University of Notre Dame Press, 1970), p. 107–127.

6. In his discussion of Poe's use of first-person narrative, Jonathan Auerbach suggests that the very enunciation of the self's "I" in a Poe story sets the stage for the self's destruction. See *The Romance of Failure: First-Person Fictions of Poe, Hawthorne, and James* (New York: Oxford University Press, 1989), 20–70.

7. For a detailed analysis of structural and narrative similarities between *Pym*'s first and second parts, see Kenneth Silverman, *Edgar A. Poe: Mournful and Never-ending Remembrance* (New York: Harper Collins Publishers, 1991), 473–474.

8. David Ketterer discusses Arthur's affinities for Poe's aesthetic theory in *The Rationale of Deception in Poe* (Baton Rouge: Louisiana State University Press, 1979), 128.

119
Notes to
Pages 70–80

9. Edgar Allan Poe, *The Narrative of Arthur Gordon Pym of Nantucket*, ed. Harold Beaver (Middlesex: Penguin Books, 1975), 57. All further references to this edition will be noted in the text.

10. Patrick F. Quinn discusses what he calls the novel's "pattern of recurrent revolt" in *The French Face of Edgar Poe* (Carbondale: Southern Illinois University Press, 1957), 169–215.

11. Edward H. Davidson discusses the salvation of deceit and disguise for Pym in *Poe: A Critical Study* (Cambridge, Mass.: Harvard University Press, 1957), 156–180.

12. Edgar Allan Poe, "Marginalia," in *Essays and Reviews*, ed. Thompson, 1313.

13. See, for example, Daniel Hoffman, *Poe, Poe, Poe, Poe, Poe, Poe, Poe* (New York: Vintage Books, 1972), 269. Hoffman also considers that the "rational" side of Poe's characters always seeks its own self-destruction. As he explains, each of Poe's major characters suffers "the longing of the perpetrator of a perfect crime to reveal his own iniquity. It is *the longing of the living body to die*, of the organic to become inorganic, of the differentiated consciousness in the agony of its separateness to experience the frightening ecstasy of its reintegration into the unity from which it has been exiled— the unity of personal annihilation" (268).

14. The best psychoanalytical interpretation of Poe's work remains Marie Bonaparte's *The Life and Works of Edgar Allan Poe: A Psychoanalytic Interpretation*, trans. John Rodker (New York: Humanities Press, 1971).

15. J. Gerald Kennedy, *Poe, Death, and the Life of Writing* (New Haven: Yale University Press, 1987), 156. In the full passage, Kennedy explains that "Poe inscribes the idea of providential order only to erase it with an instance of deception, violence, or death. The ship which seems to promise the castaways a 'glorious deliverance,' thereby furnishing a sign of God's mercy, reveals itself as a ghastly emblem of their corporeal fate."

16. Charles Feidelson, Jr., *Symbolism and American Literature* (1953; Chicago and London: University of Chicago Press, 1983), 39.

17. Evelyn J. Hinz, "'Tekeli-li': *The Narrative of Arthur Gordon Pym* as Satire," *Genre* 3 (1970): 379–399. Hinz compares Arthur with the Prefect G——, absurdly "measuring the dimensions of the chasms in incredible detail" while the imaginative act of interpretation is left to the editor, Poe, rather than the detective, Dupin (384).

18. Poe, *Letters*, ed. Ostrom, 2: 427–428.

19. Ibid., 1: 256–257.

20. Josiah C. Nott, "Two Lectures on the Natural History of the Caucasian and Negro Races," in *The Ideology of Slavery: Proslavery*

Thought in the Antebellum South, 1830–1860, ed. Drew Gilpin Faust (Baton Rouge: Louisiana State University Press, 1981), 237.

21. For an excellent discussion of the effect of contemporary slave revolts on Poe's novel, see Harold Beaver's introduction to *Pym* in the edition noted above, particularly pages 14–26. Also see Walter E. Bezanson, "The Troubled Sleep of Arthur Gordon Pym," in *Essays in Literary History: Presented to J. Milton French*, ed. Rudolf Kirk and C. F. Main (New Jersey: Rutgers University Press, 1960), 149–175.

22. For this reason I don't agree with Dennis Pahl, who claims that the multiple misreadings of the runes creates an atmosphere in which the reader learns to suspect that "any sort of authority must remain questionable." Poe considers his own authority indisputable and a secret his dumb readers have no right to comprehend. See Dennis Pahl, *Architects of the Abyss: The Indeterminate Fictions of Poe, Hawthorne, and Melville* (Columbia: University of Missouri Press, 1989), 47–56.

23. John Carlos Rowe, *Through the Custom House: Nineteenth-Century American Fiction and Modern Theory* (Baltimore: Johns Hopkins University Press, 1982), 99. Poe's theory of language, as well as his novel, is extensively discussed by John T. Irwin, *American Hieroglyphics: The Symbol of the Egyptian Hieroglyphics in the American Renaissance* (Baltimore: Johns Hopkins University Press, 1980), 43–235. The best discussion of the distinctions between "black" and "white" in the novel are discussed by Charles O'Donnel, "From Earth to Ether: Poe's Flight into Space," *PMLA* 77 (1962): 85–91. O'Donnel sees the oppositions in color as an opposition of different worlds: "Blackness or darkness is therefore associated with the desire to live in man's present condition on earth; it is the life wish—but a wish for 'the primitive life on earth' rather than 'the ultimate life of Heaven.'"

24. See Harry Levin, *The Power of Blackness: Hawthorne, Poe, Melville* (New York: Vintage Books, 1958), 122. For his discussion of Poe's anxieties about the democratic mob and black slaves, I'm indebted to Levin's chapters on Poe in their entirety.

25. While I agree with the various contemporary critics that *Pym* stands as a sort of metafictional precursor, I think Poe's "game," unlike the games of Nabokov or Barth, is played entirely at the reader's expense. In his *persona* as *Pym*'s "editor," Poe pretends to be baffled by the cavern's runes not because he wants to open up a free play of signification but because he wants to mock the stupid readers who don't "get it." For readings of *Pym* as an elaborate "metafictional classic" which helps reader and writer "embrace" at the end, see Henry F. Smith, "P/P . . . Tekelili: *Pym* Decoded,"

English Studies in Canada 14, no. 1 (March 1988): 82–93; or Joseph G. Kronick, "Edgar Allan Poe: The Error of Reading and the Reading of Error," in *Southern Literature and Literary Theory*, ed. Jefferson Humphries (Athens and London: University of Georgia Press, 1990), 206–225.

26. Poe, *Essays and Reviews*, ed. Thompson, 820.

27. Edgar Allan Poe, "Review of *Slavery in the United States*," in *The Complete Works of Edgar Allan Poe*, ed. James A. Harrison (1902; New York: AMS Press, 1965), 8: 266.

28. Edgar Allan Poe, "Eureka," in *The Science Fiction of Edgar Allan Poe*, ed. Harold Beaver (Middlesex: Penguin Books, 1976), 248.

29. Levin, *The Power of Blackness*, 121.

30. Vincent Buranelli, *Edgar Allan Poe*, 2d ed. (Boston: Twayne Publishers, 1977), 59.

31. Edgar Allan Poe, "The Philosophy of Composition," in *Essays and Reviews*, ed. Thompson, 17.

32. The redemptive power of destruction, as well as Usher's affinity with the cosmology outlined in *Eureka*, is discussed at great length by Maurice Beebe, "The Universe of Roderick Usher," in *Poe: A Collection of Critical Essays*, ed. Robert Regan (New Jersey: Prentice Hall, 1967), 121–133.

33. Edgar Allan Poe, "Letter to B——," in *Essays and Reviews*, ed. Thompson, 6.

34. Edgar Allan Poe, "Review of *Twice-Told Tales*," in ibid., 571.

35. Stephen Railton, *Authorship and Audience: Literary Performance in the American Renaissance* (Princeton: Princeton University Press, 1991), 138.

36. Edgar Allan Poe, "The Philosophy of Furniture," in *The Works of Edgar Allan Poe in Eight Volumes* (Philadelphia: J. B. Lippincott Co., 1845), 6: 50.

37. Edgar Allan Poe, "The Power of Words," in *The Science Fiction of Edgar Allan Poe*, ed. Beaver, 174.

38. Edgar Allan Poe, "Anastatic Printing," in *The Works of Edgar Allan Poe*, 6: 259.

39. Shoshana Felman, "On Reading Poetry: Reflections on the Limits and Possibilities of Psychoanalytical Approaches," in *Modern Critical Views: Edgar Allan Poe*, ed. Harold Bloom (New York: Chelsea House Publishers, 1985), 137. Also see Jacques Lacan, "Seminar on 'The Purloined Letter,'" trans. Jeffrey Mehlman, *Yale French Studies* 48 (1972): 38–72; John T. Irwin, "Mysteries We Reread, Mysteries of Rereading: Poe, Borges, and the Analytic Detective Story; Also Lacan, Derrida, and Johnson," *MLN* 101 (1986): 1168–1215.

40. As Donald E. Pease writes: "In Poe's works . . . words disintegrate

into letters, sheer material impressions bereft of their power to represent. Poe thereby breaks the verbal contract constitutive of a culture of individuals. In the process of writing, he produces words without the power to refer and persons without the power to reflect and thereby empties persons and characters out of the actual world and into a world of memory" (*Visionary Compacts: American Renaissance Writings in Cultural Context* [Madison: University of Wisconsin Press, 1987], 188). Pease's argument complements Silverman's in that they both see Poe using form and metrics to reduce all language to a sort of ritual incantation, a memory of primal unity which existed before words came along to distinguish everybody from one another. I think Pease and Silverman are very probably right.

41. Michel Foucault, *Discipline and Punish: The Birth of the Prison*, trans. Alan Sheridan (New York: Vintage Books, 1979), 208.

Index